I0937122

The Story of Mexico

Benito Juárez
and the
French Intervention

The Story of Mexico

Benito Juárez
and the
French Intervention

R. Conrad Stein

MORGAN
REYNOLDS
PUBLISHING

Greensboro, North Carolina

The Story of Mexico

Benito Juárez and the French Intervention

The Mexican Revolution

The Mexican War of Independence

Cortés and the Spanish Conquest

THE STORY OF MEXICO
BENITO JUÁREZ AND THE FRENCH INTERVENTION

Copyright © 2008 by R. Conrad Stein

Library of Congress Cataloging-in-Publication Data

Stein, R. Conrad.
    The story of Mexico : Benito Juarez and the French intervention / by R. Conrad Stein.
        p. cm.
    Includes bibliographical references and index.
    ISBN-13: 978-1-59935-052-3
    ISBN-10: 1-59935-052-1
    1. Juarez, Benito, 1806-1872. 2. Mexico--History--1821-1861. 3. Mexico--History--European intervention, 1861-1867. 4. Mexico--History--1867-1910. I. Title. II. Title: Benito Juarez and the French intervention.
    F1233.J9S74 2007
    972'.07092--dc22
    [B]
                                        2007016005

Printed in the United States of America
First Edition

For my wife Deborah and daughter, Janna

Contents

Benito Juárez
(Courtesy of The Granger Collection)

ONE

The Student Meets the General

xcitement gripped the city of Oaxaca (pronounced wah-HAH-cah) in southern Mexico as the people prepared to greet a very important visitor. It was December 1829, less than ten years after Mexico had won its independence from Spain. The infant nation was in a perilous position. European powers such as France, England, and the former mother country—Spain—threatened to invade Mexico's shores. Mexico's northern neighbor, the United States, grew more powerful every year. In addition to the foreign threats, the nation was being torn from within by civil wars and army uprisings.

The visitor coming to Oaxaca loomed as the one strongman who could save Mexico from its many enemies. He was Antonio López de Santa Anna, an army general with ambitions to gain high political office. Three years earlier General Santa Anna had driven a Spanish army out of the port city of Tampico. Actually the Spanish soldiers were weakened by an epidemic of yellow fever, and were already in the process of sailing away from the port. Still, Santa Anna took credit for a victory and he was hailed as the "Hero of Tampico."

Now the Hero entered a Oaxaca hall where he was to be given a formal dinner. College students waited on tables for Santa Anna and his staff. By chance a young, dark-skinned Indian student was assigned to Santa Anna's table. Santa Anna was a white man. Customs dictated that Indians were not even to look a white person in the eye when conversing with him. Indians were expected to drop their gaze and stare rather dumbly at the ground during any interaction with whites.

It is not known if the Indian student dropped his gaze when he waited on Santa Anna's table. In the future the student said and wrote very little about the incident. Santa Anna looked not at his waiter's face but at his feet. The student was barefoot. This impoverished Indian youth could not even afford to buy a pair of shoes. Years later Santa Anna bitterly wrote, "with his bare feet on the floor . . . It is amazing that an Indian of such low degree should have become the figure in Mexico that we all know."

The college student who acted as Santa Anna's waiter that night was Benito Juárez. He rose to become president of his country during a time of turmoil and bloody civil war. He led Mexico to victory over invaders from France. Juárez became one of the most beloved figures in all of Mexican history. As president he tried—though he did not succeed— to bring democracy and worldwide respect to Mexico. His ideas outlived the man. Today Mexicans look upon Juárez in the same light as Americans see George Washington or Abraham Lincoln. Benito Juárez laid the foundation for the modern Republic of Mexico.

TWO

The Zapotec Shepherd Boy

Benito Juárez was born March 21, 1806, in the village of San Pablo Guelatao, in the state of Oaxaca. Less than twenty-four hours after he was born his parents wrapped him in blankets and took him to church to be baptized. The church listed his name on the record books as Benito Pablo Juárez. There was a reason why his baptism took place so shortly after his birth. Disease and sudden death struck babies with brutal frequency in Mexico. His parents wanted the baby to be baptized immediately so if he died he would enter the afterlife as a proper Christian.

Death was no stranger in the Juárez household. When Benito was only three years old both his parents died. His father dropped dead while selling fruit in a market. His mother died giving birth to a younger sister. Benito and his two older sisters went to live with their grandparents, but they too died in a few years. Poverty, hunger, and diseases such as smallpox and yellow fever took many lives in Mexican

This map shows the Mexican state of Oaxaca, the birthplace of Juárez.

communities. Because of the raging sicknesses, orphans were common. Usually the orphans were absorbed into the families of relatives.

Benito came under the care of his uncle Bemardino Juárez. The uncle was a bachelor, and man and boy lived in a little hut on the outskirts of town. Juárez described his village as a tiny place holding about twenty families. The village people were uneducated and impoverished. Most of his neighbors were unable even to write their own names on paper.

Juárez entertained mixed feelings about his uncle. Always he wrote respectably about the man in his diary. But a short biography written during his lifetime claimed the uncle, "treated him badly and gave him little care." Juárez reviewed that biography carefully and changed much of the writing.

However he did not edit out the sentence indicating his uncle's maltreatment.

Almost everyone in San Pablo Guelatao was a Zapotec Indian. The Zapotecs were a proud nation which thrived in southern Mexico and Central America from 500 BC to 1500 AD. Even after Spain conquered Mexico in the early 1500s, the Zapotecs never acted the part of a captive people. They lived quietly with little change in their routine despite the flags of Spain fluttering over their lands.

The Zapotec Indians flourished in Central Mexico from 500 BC until 1500 AD.

The state of Oaxaca, in southern Mexico, was made up principally of Zapotec and Mixtec Indians. Most Zapotecs preferred to speak their old language. Juárez said about his village, "the Spanish language was hardly ever spoken." Older people among the Zapotecs secretly worshiped their ancient gods, even though Catholic priests condemned such worship as a mortal sin.

The Juárez family, though poor, were leaders in the Zapotec village. Adults in the family were said to be the silent and serious type, a class of people who enjoyed great respect. Ancient laws and traditions said only important families were allowed to earn their livings through the ownership of animals. Uncle Bemardino Juárez owned a herd of sheep, giving him a high status in the village. Benito naturally assumed his uncle's profession and became a shepherd.

At the age of fifty, Juárez wrote the autobiographical *Notes For My Children*. It was a short book detailing his

Monte Alban

Some fifteen hundred years ago the Zapotecs built a magnificent temple complex called Monte Alban just outside of the present day city of Oaxaca. During its time of glory the complex served as a religious and political capital for more than 100,000 people.

Monte Alban spread over a mountain top that was laboriously leveled by ancient workmen. On the level area rose pyramids, tombs, and ball courts upon which teams played an ancient game similar to soccer. Featured inside one of the earliest structures is a series of carvings of men who appear to be dancing.

Today visitors arrive by busloads to marvel at the great engineering and artistic skill displayed by the long ago Zapotec people who built Monte Alban.

An aerial view of Monte Alban

life to date with special emphasis on his early years. The book's style reveals the personality of its author. *Notes* is written with matter-of-fact precision and is devoid of flowery language. Because he writes without passion it is difficult to discern whether Juárez considered himself happy or unhappy as a boy. About going to live with his uncle at a young age he said simply, "I was left under the care of my uncle Bemardino Juárez because my other uncles . . . had already died." Further on he remarks, "as soon as I could think at all, I dedicated myself, insofar as my tender age permitted, to work in the fields."

His boyhood was lonely. He grew up with his bachelor uncle and without brothers and sisters in his immediate household.

Young Benito probably had little contact with women. Also the job of being a shepherd is a solitary one. He spent his days and a good part of his evenings on the mountain slopes tending to a small herd of sheep which no doubt included a cow or two. As a boy Juárez thought about becoming a priest. To practice for his future vocation he sometimes climbed a tree and delivered sermons to his flock of animals.

Describing the boy Benito Juárez, a relation wrote, "his character was obedient, reserved in his thoughts, and in general withdrawn. He had friends, but few, and with them was formal and showed good judgment." In many regards the boy acted similar to the man who would later rule Mexico. Young Juárez was serious, deep-thinking, and at times joyless. But he also possessed a curious intellect which forever drove him to accept new challenges and make new discoveries.

Dominating his *Notes For My Children* was his desire to obtain an education. There was no school in the town, so Benito turned to his uncle for the learning experience. Reflecting the family's position of leadership, Uncle Bemardino had learned to read and write in passable Spanish. In *Notes* Juárez wrote, "In the few spare moments in which we were not working, my uncle taught me to read." Benito was his own toughest task master, "when my uncle called me to give me my lesson, I myself took him the switch, so that he could beat me with it if I didn't know the lesson."

His uncle urged Benito to become a Catholic priest. The priesthood was considered an honored profession, one which reflected a man with learning and wisdom. Being a priest was also one of the only ways an impoverished Indian could seek employment other than in farm fields. As Juárez wrote, "back then it was very difficult for poor people, and especially for Indians, to follow any learned career except through the church."

Aside from family, the church was the most powerful influence on the lives of Mexican people. The church set the rhythms and order of village life. Church bells called the people to mass and announced births, deaths, and marriages. Grand festivals were held in churchyards. The church provided art with its paintings and sculptures. People took their troubles as well as their illnesses to church where they prayed for relief from suffering. Benito Juárez believed with all his heart in the righteousness of the church and in the miracle of God's creation. Becoming a priest would celebrate his love for Catholicism.

When he was twelve an incident took place that shaped his life. His job as a shepherd boy was mainly to keep his animals from eating the corn crops and the vegetable gardens planted by his neighbors. Theft of animals was not a problem. Indian people of rural Mexico were scrupulously honest and respected each other's property. So Benito was not alarmed when a band of travelers walked the road outside of town and paused to talk with him. The travelers had recently visited the city of Oaxaca, a place he longed to see someday.

Benito had no idea he was being tricked. As he talked to one traveler, another stole one of his sheep. When the boy discovered the loss he was shocked and terrified. His uncle was bedeviled by a raging temper. Benito Juárez had a scar above his lip that was evident even when he was an old man. Some biographers have concluded the scar was put there by a beating given to him by his uncle during one of the man's tantrums. Now he dreaded how the uncle would

When Juárez was twelve years old, he ran away from the small village of San Pablo Guelatao to the large city of Oaxaca, where he lived as a houseboy in this house.

react to the loss of a sheep, a loss caused by the shepherd boy's carelessness.

Benito decided to run away. Far away over mountain roads lay the city of Oaxaca. The big city held schools where he could continue his education. In *Notes* he does not say his move was an act of flight made to escape punishment from his uncle. Instead he claimed he voluntarily walked to Oaxaca for the education opportunities the city afforded: "I believed that I could learn only by going to the city."

Oaxaca loomed as the greatest change-of-life chapter in Benito's life. He loved—as well as feared—his uncle and knew he would miss the man. He would also miss his familiar house and all his friends. Oaxaca was a city where rich white people lived. He had rarely seen a white person. People in the city spoke Spanish, and he knew only a few halting words of that language.

The Races of Mexico

Mexico is a multiracial society, and the issue of race is also complex. The vast majority of people in Mexico are *mestizos*, meaning mixed race. But the country is also home to *indios*, (Indians, the indigenous people of Mexico), *negros*, (blacks, tens of thousands of whom were brought by the Spanish as slaves), and whites. White is generally used to describe Spaniards, and any non-Spanish whites are generally labeled by nationality rather than race: American, German, British, etc.

Of his tangled feelings before setting out to the city he said,

Also, I too was hesitant to separate myself from [my uncle], to leave the house that sheltered me in my orphaned childhood, and to abandon my little friends, with whom I had always had the deepest sympathies and from whom any separation always hurt me. The conflict that arose within me, between these feelings and my desire to go to another society, new and unknown to me, where I might acquire an education, was cruel indeed. However, my hunger [to get an education] overcame my fears, and on December 17, 1818, when I was twelve years old, I fled from my house and walked to the city of Oaxaca.

Benito took to the road, probably carrying little more than one change of clothes. He ate wild berries along the way. Juárez claimed he made the entire twenty-five mile trip in one day and arrived the same night. If true it was an incredibly brisk hike over mountain trails and taken by a twelve-year-old who was quite possibly barefoot at the time.

Locked in his mind was the germ of a plan. One of his sisters worked as a housemaid and cook in the city. Benito hoped to get temporary lodging with her and then seek employment on his own. His ultimate goal was to enter an academy and work his way through school. The plan unfolded with an almost miraculous precision.

María Josepha, his sister, was older than Benito. They did not live together as they were put in different households after the death of their parents, but they were close. She was an independent teenager who had the misfortune of marrying young to an alcoholic. She escaped her drunken husband and moved to Oaxaca two years earlier to start a new life. In the city, she worked for the family of Don Antonio Maza. Maza, a white man of Italian heritage, was a wealthy dealer of groceries and other goods.

Benito found the Maza house right away. He and his sister fell into each other's arms. They had not seen each other for many months. The head of the household, Don Antonio Maza, agreed to let Benito sleep in a spare room in return for household chores. The Maza family would later play a vital role in his life. Connecting with his sister and the Maza's was a stroke of luck for the shepherd boy who ventured into the city. He soon had another brush with good fortune when he met a man who became, in the Spanish tradition, his godfather.

"There lived in the city, then, a pious and very honorable man who worked as a bookbinder," wrote Juárez in *Notes For My Children*. The meeting with the bookbinder was probably arranged by the Maza family. He was Antonio Salanueva, an unmarried white man of Spanish background and a devoted Catholic. Benito joined the Salanueva household and worked as a houseboy. He slept on a straw mat in the bookbinder shop which stood in front of the house. His tasks included washing floors, building the fire, and watering the many plants. With satisfaction, Benito Juárez wrote, "In this manner I found myself settled in Oaxaca on January 7, 1819."

Salanueva became the father Benito never knew. Benito entered the man's heart as his only son. The bookbinder sponsored Benito through the process of confirmation, the holy ceremony where a boy reaffirms his commitment to the church. After confirmation Salanueva became Benito's godfather according to Catholic law. The love between the two grew, and they lived in a happy house.

Benito struggled with learning the Spanish language. Spanish lessons given by his uncle did not prepare him to live in this new world. He later wrote, "I spoke the Spanish language without rules and with all the errors made by the uneducated." The learning process was slow. Every day Benito memorized new words and phrases. There were many other Zapotec-speaking people in town, yet he forced himself to speak Spanish only. Eventually he became fluent, but his difficulties in learning Spanish caused him embarrassment. As he grew older he was known as a person who was almost stony quiet. Perhaps his early problems in mastering Spanish contributed to his silent demeanor.

Antonio Salanueva believed every bright young person deserved a proper education. Rarely had he seen a student more eager or hardworking than Benito Juárez. At first the

The Benito Juárez House

The house where Juárez lived with Antonio Salanueva has been preserved and can be toured today in the city of Oaxaca. Visitors see the patio where Benito dutifully watered the plants. They also walk through the bookbinding workshop, complete with vintage tools. There Benito and his godfather once bound and repaired books.

bookbinder patiently taught the boy to read in their spare time at home. Salanueva had a profound respect for books and for scholarship. Avidly the man read and reread the Epistles (letters) of St. Paul in the Bible. Another of Salanueva's favorite authors was a Spanish monk named Feijóo who was a pioneer educator in Spain. Benito Juárez too fell in love with books, a love he maintained his entire life.

When he had free time Benito explored his town. Oaxaca was the capital of the state of the same name. It was a world different from the village where Benito was born. Holding about 25,000 people, it was Mexico's fourth-largest city. Fountains bubbled in the town's lush public gardens. Mansions surrounded by high walls sheltered the families of the rich whites. Zapotec and Mixtec Indians made up the bulk of the city's population. The Indians ran the colorful markets which served as the town's social centers. Vendors displayed fruit and vegetables in the markets. Small shops sold bright woven blankets and expertly carved wooden statues of the Catholic saints, all made by Indian artists.

Oaxaca was famous for its churches. The Mexican historian Justo Sierra, who lived in Juárez' time, said, "Oaxaca was a city that lived in the shadow of a monastery. There everyone was a friar or wanted to be one." Just two blocks from Benito's house rose the spires of Santo Domingo, one of the most strikingly beautiful churches in all Mexico.

The church-sponsored festivals and pageants were especially passionate in Oaxaca. The Easter ceremony was both sad and triumphant as it represented death followed by resurrection. Guadalupe Day, December 12, was a day of joy when Mexicans honored their patron saint. During festival days Indians from the ranches streamed into town causing the

The Santo Domingo church, one of the most majestic and famous in Oaxaca, was located just two blocks from Juárez's house.

population to double. Parades of men carried litters bearing the statues of saints. The long processions wound through the streets. Flute players and people beating on drums accompanied the marchers. All classes of the city—the beggars as well as the bankers—were swept up with the excitement of *fiesta*.

At the Council Seminary Juárez studied Latin, theology, and other subjects needed to ready him for the priesthood. Secretly, he was beginning to entertain doubts as to whether he would be a good priest or even if he would enjoy the calling. He was especially dismayed at how the student priests were taught at the seminary where lessons emphasized memorization and the recitation of memorized words and phrases. Teachers did little to encourage reason or original thought from their students. Juárez wrote, "I was dissatisfied with this deplorable method of teaching." His belief in God and in the goodness of the church was absolute. The men who had so far influenced his life—his uncle, his godfather, and Antonio Maza—all encouraged him to become a priest. So he continued to study for the priesthood because he could not disappoint those men who had given him so much.

His best friend at school was a frail young man named Miguel Mendez. This friend, who died when he was in his early twenties, knew Juárez well enough to understand he was pondering a career other than the priesthood. Mendez was the first to predict a bright future for young Benito. At a graduation dinner Mendez turned to Juárez, raised his glass and said, "And this one whom you see here, so serious and reserved, this one will be a great politician. He will rise higher than any of us, and he will be one of our great men and [bring] glory to our country."

THREE

Independence and a New Mexico

In the early 1800s a forbidden word—independence—was whispered among Mexican intellectuals. Soon the whispers became a roar. This idea sweeping Mexico was new and bold. All Mexicans understood any independence movement meant certain war with Spain, one of the world's great powers.

For three hundred years Spain governed Mexico with iron rules and absolute authority. Spanish control began in 1519 when a determined soldier named Hernan Cortés landed on Mexican shores and began a war of conquest against the dominant Aztec people. Cortés brought with him horses, cannons, and a force of 650 men. The Aztec army was large and its soldiers brave, however the Spaniards enjoyed advantages in battle. The Mexicans had never before seen firearms nor had they seen horses. At first many Aztecs believed the horse and the rider perched on its back were one in the same beast, a creature out of a fantastic nightmare. The Spanish

Hernan Cortés *(Library of Congress)*

soldiers also carried a weapon they did not know they possessed: diseases such as smallpox, typhus, and diphtheria. These sicknesses had been in Europe for generations, and Spaniards developed limited immunities to them. The Indians of the Americas had no such immunities. A host of new diseases killed Aztecs by the thousands and severely weakened their ability to fight the Spaniards.

After a series of terrible battles Cortés overwhelmed the Aztecs in Mexico City (then called Tenochtitlán) and claimed all of Mexico for the Spanish king. The last battles in the Mexico City region were fought in 1521. Mexico was now a Spanish colony.

The Spaniards called their overseas colony New Spain. After it was established, settlers from Spain poured in bringing with them the Spanish language and the Catholic religion. Villages were built in the Spanish style with a church, a plaza, and a market in the center of town.

Under Spanish rule the Mexican people divided into three classes: the whites, the mestizos (a mixture between Indians and whites), and the Indians. Whites led the government and dominated New Spain's economy. The mestizos were given limited privileges by the white ruling class. Indians had little share in government or in business.

New Spain was a fabulously rich colony. Some 5000 silver mines operated and produced thousands of tons of the precious metal. Gold and silver taken from New Spain helped the Spanish government build a mighty fleet of warships which further enhanced the worldwide Spanish empire. Despite this wealth, the bulk of New Spain's people were impoverished. Mines were worked by Indians and mestizos who labored long hours often in waist-high water. The mine workers barely earned enough to eat. If the laborers refused to work they could be tied up and whipped by the Spanish bosses.

Authorities kept New Spain a closed society. No one was allowed to worship in any church other than the Catholic Church. Immigration by foreigners, except those approved by the government, was forbidden. Books and newspapers were censored by the government as well as by the church. Free discussions and the exchange of new ideas between people were discouraged by officials.

While the colony of New Spain slept under imposed isolation, much of the rest of the world rose to answer a new call of freedom. Beginning in the 1600s, a period called the

Enlightenment, or the Age of Reason, began in Europe. This was a philosophical movement whose leaders believed humans were unique in that they alone had the ability to reason. Because people could reason, they no longer had to accept without question the orders issued by their church or their king. The English philosopher John Locke (1632–1704), who was a towering figure during the Enlightenment, declared that a government's prime responsibility was to protect human rights. If a government failed in that responsibility, Locke believed the people were justified in finding new rulers. In France, Jean Jacques Rousseau (1712-1778) wrote that people should control their governments rather than be controlled by civil authorities.

Fresh philosophical ideas became political movements. In turn, the political movements toppled governments and changed history. The Americans Thomas Jefferson and John Adams read Locke and urged their countrymen to declare independence from England in 1776. French people, who long lived under the harsh rule of a king and the upper classes, followed the American example and revolted against their government in 1789.

John Locke

The cry for change which thundered in the outside world slowly began to be heard in the closed society of New

The American Revolution (left) and French Revolution influenced a Mexican independence movement in the early nineteenth century.

Spain. Books from France which preached freedom were smuggled into the Spanish colony. Copies of the American Declaration of Independence were read in secret.

The philosophical literature entering Mexico was absorbed principally by whites. Wealthy whites knew how to read, while basic education was denied mestizos and Indians. The whites also enjoyed greater freedom to become involved in government. By the early 1800s thousands of whites were born and had lived for many generations in the Americas. Those whites, born and reared in Mexico, were called the Creoles. As the generations passed, the Creoles began to look upon Spain as a foreign country. Spain was the mother of Mexico, but it lay 4000 miles across the waters and required a voyage of many weeks to reach. Creoles questioned why the far away Spanish king should have so much power over their lives. It was the Creoles, assisted by mestizos and Indians, who led the Mexican independence movement.

On the evening of September 15, 1810, a Creole priest named Miguel Hidalgo y Costilla rang his church bell as if to summon his parishioners in for mass. When the people arrived, Father Hidalgo stood on his church steps and called for them to rise up in revolution. This historic event took place in the central Mexican town of Dolores (now called Dolores Hidalgo). It marked the start of the Mexican War of Independence.

The army of farmers led by Hidalgo was made up mostly of Indians and mestizos. Many of Hidalgo's soldiers were barefoot and armed only with clubs and machetes. Rage was their most powerful weapon. After suffering genera-tions of abuse the peasant soldiers fought as much to wreak revenge on the rich whites as they did for independence. The army became a mob. Hidalgo's men looted and burned the city of Guanajuato killing many of the residents, especially the whites. Shocked and sickened by this violence, Father Hidalgo lost heart in the cause he started. Hidalgo was captured

Miguel Hidalgo y Costilla was the first to initiate a coup against Spanish rule of Mexico. *(Library of Congress)*

by Spanish soldiers, and after a hasty trial he was executed in 1811.

After Hidalgo's death the cause of independence was taken up by José María Morelos, a mestizo priest. Morelos preached independence, but he had an even broader program. He envisioned a new government where all Mexicans—whites, mestizos, and Indians—would enjoy equality under the law. José María Morelos became a hero to the young Benito Juárez. Justo Sierra said, "You had to hear Juárez say, 'el Señor Morelos' to understand the extraordinary tradition of devotion [he had for the man]." Many whites feared they would lose their privileges under a Morelos government and they refused to support him. Morelos was captured and he too was executed by a firing squad in 1815.

The Mexicans won their independence in February 1821. By that time Spain was weakened due to a war with France.

The Mexican flag that is in use today was adopted in 1821, the year the nation won its independence. It is a tricolor banner made up of green, white, and red stripes. Green stands for independence, white for the purity of the Catholic religion, and red for unity.

Also the Enlightenment caused political upheaval in Spain. Many Spaniards became reluctant to follow the orders of their king. Pressures from within and without so crippled the government that Spain could no longer hold on to its rebellious colony, Mexico.

The independence gained by Mexico did not lead to a new and democratic society as envisioned by Morelos and Father Hidalgo. Instead the Mexican state was headed by a Spaniard named Iturbide who declared himself emperor. Iturbide had no direct ties with Spain, but his government was a profound disappointment to Mexican idealists. Mexico

Iturbide

had simply exchanged Spanish rule for the rule of a self-proclaimed emperor.

Still, the ideas of the Enlightenment that triggered world-wide revolutions remained entrenched in Mexico. Those Mexicans who embraced the policies of Locke, Rousseau, and Jefferson were generally called liberals. The liberals believed democracy was the only acceptable form of government. Opposed to the liberals stood the conservatives who felt kings and aristocrats should properly lead the masses. This liberal-versus-conservative argument was waged in many countries in the early 1800s. In Mexico the argument escalated into civil war.

Benito Juárez read the philosophical literature of the times and chose to join the liberals. In fact, the liberal system of beliefs changed his choice of study and helped to decide his future career. Young Juárez was not a happy student at the Council Seminary because the school created what were called "mass and meal" priests. These were priests who knew Latin versus well enough to chant the words of a mass. In return for celebrating a mass they were given a simple meal. Juárez said, "[They] could only say mass to earn a living, and were not permitted to preach or to exercise any other functions requiring instruction and ability."

In 1827 a new college, the Institute of Science and Arts, opened in Oaxaca. The school was established by the liberal party. Some of its teachers were priests, but the college was not sanctioned by the church. For Juárez the school offered exciting courses in science and philosophy. To attend the Institute of Science and Arts he would have to quit the Council Seminary and denounce any plans he had to become a priest. His godfather, Antonio Salanueva, was disappointed when Juárez decided to abandon the priesthood. But above all Salanueva supported education. He knew Juárez was not quitting school. He was simply changing courses, which should be part of the freedoms enjoyed by any serious student. In August 1828 Juárez entered the Institute of Science and Arts to begin the study of law.

Less than a year later, Benito Juárez had his memorable encounter with Antonio López de Santa Anna by waiting on the general's table. Juárez knew Santa Anna by reputation. When the general visited Oaxaca he was already a powerful man, poised to take his place in Mexican history.

GENERAL D. ANTONIO LOPEZ DE SANTA-ANNA.
PRESIDENT OF THE REPUBLIC OF MEXICO.
By A. Hoffy, from an original likeness taken from life at Vera-Cruz.

Antonio López de Santa Anna

Scholars often called the 1830s and 1840s the Age of Santa Anna.

Antonio López de Santa Anna was born near Veracruz on February 21, 1795, to a white and well-to-do family. At fifteen he joined the Spanish army as a cadet. Over the years he became a skilled army officer. He fought for Spain in the Mexican War of Independence. His wartime Spanish loyalties alone should have dishonored him in independent Mexico, but Santa Anna displayed a genius for self promotion. Time after time he was able to turn political and military defeats into victories simply by telling the public he had won.

Mexico suffered a series of crises after independence. Unlike its northern neighbor, the United States, Mexico had no experience with home rule. Spanish authorities jealously kept decision-making powers to themselves during the three-hundred-year-long colonial period. Because Mexicans lacked experience establishing governments, confusion and political upheavals were common in the post independence period. Between 1821 and 1850 Mexico had fifty different governments. Mostly the governments were the result of proclamations which came about when one political strongman or another rose to "proclaim" a new government.

The most opportunistic of the proclaimers was Antonio López de Santa Anna. At heart he was a conservative, however he was willing to take up the liberal label if it allowed him seize the presidential office. From 1833 to 1855 Santa Anna became Mexico's president eleven separate times. When he was not president he led the nation's armies. Often he served as both the president and the country's highest-ranking army general at the same time. Many Mexicans, upset because of their country's turmoil, accepted Santa Anna's leadership in hopes he would bring some measure of order to their government. The historian Justo Sierra said Mexicans followed Santa Anna in the same way religious people follow a man who they perceive or at least hope to be a savior: "Peoples who are accustomed to praying . . . see their successful leaders as Messiahs, whether these be true geniuses or merely men with luck."

While Mexico floundered without a stable government, the student Benito Juárez began a new course of study—law.

In the years to come he acquired an almost religious respect for the law and all it could bring to a society. He saw around him lawlessness at the national level. Generals and politicians seized control of the government without regard to the legal methods of obtaining power. Lawlessness promoted civil wars, empowered the military, and kept Mexico a backwards nation. Juárez believed a constitution—a set of written laws—ought to be every nation's highest authority. Laws, unbending and applied equally to all citizens, must guide Mexico in the future. If and when he entered politics, he would be directed by law and law alone.

The Age of Santa Anna proved disastrous for Mexico. The country's misfortunes centered on the sprawling but sparsely populated region that was loosely called Mexico's northern frontier. That area, more than a half million square

In 1839, Mexico comprised land that later became Texas, Arizona, Nevada, New Mexico, Utah, Colorado, and California. *(Library of Congress)*

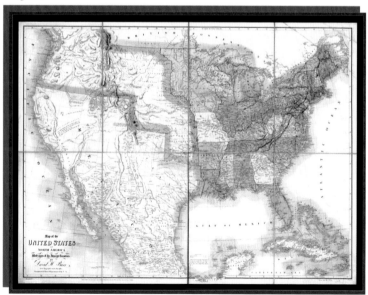

miles wide, lay above the Rio Grande River and is now part of the United States. The northern frontier included the present-day American states of Texas, New Mexico, Arizona, and California.

In 1821, Stephen Austin led a small band of settlers from the United States to the province of Texas. There the Americans established cattle ranches and cotton farms. At first they were welcomed by the Mexican government. The American settlers took oaths vowing to convert to Catholicism, learn Spanish, and become loyal Mexicans. Within ten years some 30,000 Americans had migrated to Texas, and they easily outnumbered the Mexicans living there. In 1835, the American pioneers, calling themselves Texans, split from Mexico and declared Texas to be an independent state.

In 1836, a group of Texans barricaded themselves in an old mission church in San Antonio called the Alamo. They were led by men who became legends in American history: Davy Crockett, the pioneer turned congressman; Jim Bowie, a frontiersman who is said to have invented the double edged

The Slave Question

History books in the United States often claim the Texans declared their independence from Mexico because they were lovers of freedom. This notion overlooks the fact of slavery. Many Texans had immigrated from Kentucky, Tennessee, and other southern states. They brought their slaves with them. Years earlier Mexico had abolished slavery. When the Mexican government threatened to enforce the law and free the slaves in Texas, the Texans rebelled. So, ironically, one of the "freedoms" the Texans sought was their freedom to own slaves.

This painting depicts the battle at the Alamo. *(Library of Congress)*

Bowie knife; and William Travis, an experienced soldier. According to an often told story, Travis drew a line in the sand with his sword and announced that anyone wishing to leave the Alamo and therefore escape the coming battle was free to do so. Not one man crossed the line.

Into San Antonio marched General Santa Anna and an army of 3,000 soldiers. Facing this force stood a band of about 187 Alamo defenders. As Santa Anna approached the Alamo, his troops flew a blood red flag and his buglers sounded a grim refrain called the *deguello*. The flag and song meant he intended to take no prisoners and show no mercy. The general was determined to punish the rebellious Texans and to teach a lesson to other land-hungry Yankees who might seek territory in Mexico. After bombarding the Alamo walls with artillery, Santa Anna ordered his men to storm the church on March 6, 1836. All the Alamo defenders were slaughtered. The only Americans to survive the battle were an officer's wife, her baby, a Mexican maid, and a slave boy.

After the Alamo battle an overconfident Santa Anna relaxed—literally. On the afternoon of April 21, 1836, Santa Anna camped with his troops at San Jacinto in Texas. The men and their commander took their customary afternoon nap, the siesta. Suddenly they were charged upon by Texans shouting a battle cry: "Remember the Alamo." Led by Sam Houston, the Texans overpowered their enemy in a battle that lasted only fifteen minutes. More than four hundred Mexican soldiers were killed. Many soldiers were sleeping or trying to surrender when they were cut down by the Texans.

Sam Houston

Santa Anna, disguised in the uniform of a common soldier, escaped the carnage of San Jacinto on horseback. Two days later he was captured by Sam Houston's men and was forced to sign an agreement to pull all Mexican troops out of Texas. Santa Anna then returned to Mexico in shame; however his period of disgrace was short-lived. In December 1838, Santa Anna led Mexican soldiers trying to dislodge French troops who had taken over the port city of Veracruz. In an exchange of gunfire a cannonball tore off his right leg. Santa Anna, sensing the publicity value of the wound, gave his severed leg a military funeral. The theatrics worked, and Santa Anna became Mexico's darling once more.

The Pastry War

The 1838 battle at Veracruz where Santa Anna lost his leg was part of a minor engagement stemming from Mexico's failure to pay certain debts to France. One of the debts was to a French pastry chef who claimed that Mexican soldiers ate his cakes and refused to pay for them. Mexican writers dubbed the conflict the "Pastry War."

As president, Santa Anna entertained foreign dignitaries by staging dress balls and hosting elaborate state dinners. He built the largest theater in the world and called it, appropriately, *El Teatro de Santa Anna*. These pet projects cost the Mexican treasury a fortune. To raise funds Santa Anna imposed novel and sometimes bizarre taxes on his people. Mexican property owners were taxed based on how many windows they had on their houses. Taxes were also levied on the length of a homeowner's rain gutters, and even on how many dogs the owner kept.

Benito Juárez finished his courses and became a lawyer in 1831. Mexico was in a state of terrible disorder, but the twenty-five-year-old attorney concentrated on establishing himself in his new profession. He was already a respected young man in the community based on his record at the Institute of Science and Arts. The school promoted him to professor and he taught a course in physics. Also in 1831, he was elected to the post of alderman for the city of Oaxaca. An alderman heads a neighborhood government unit, and by taking this position he started his political career.

One of his first cases as a lawyer came when Indian farmers from a nearby town asked him to intervene in a dispute with a parish priest. The farmers said the priest charged high rates for services such as Baptism and church marriages. Juárez agreed to represent the farmers, and by doing so he angered certain powerful politicians. He was promptly put in jail after a magistrate claimed he urged poor people to overthrow their government. Juárez remained in jail for nine days. He learned the consequences of challenging authority, but he continued his work to bring the purity of law to his community. Juárez firmly believed that laws, if properly applied, would promote fairness to those on the bottom level of society and civility to those on top.

Slowly, Juárez advanced in Oaxaca society. In 1833, he was elected as a deputy in the state legislature. It must be noted that in those days only minor public officials, called electors, were permitted to vote. The vast majority of Mexicans were illiterate and forbidden to vote because they could not read the names on a ballot. In addition to holding political offices, Juárez wrote newspaper articles on court proceedings. Through his writings his reputation spread beyond the state of Oaxaca. Slowly legal scholars came to respect him as an authority on the law.

In his work as a lawyer Juárez naturally sympathized with the downtrodden, but he also took up the cause of wealthy landowners in matters such as property disputes. Fairness under the law was his doctrine. Rich and poor understood Benito Juárez argued cases based on the meaning of the law. Always he pushed aside his own feelings for the people involved in court proceedings.

In 1843, at the age of thirty-seven, Benito Juárez got married. Though he was a bachelor he had not been without girlfriends. He had fathered at least two illegitimate children by the time of his marriage. Such common law families were not unusual. Few people talked about his illegitimate children in public because such talk would be considered bad taste. His wife was Margarita Maza, the seventeen-year-old daughter of the Maza family. This was the same wealthy family that once employed his sister as a cook. Juárez had remained a close family friend. On visits he used to play with his future wife when she was a toddler.

Margarita was of pure European blood. A white man marrying an Indian woman was common enough in those days, but the reverse was somewhat rare. Discrimination against Indians remained an everyday practice in Mexico. In many Mexican communities, Indians were not even permitted to sit on a bench in a public park. The Maza family knew and trusted Juárez and their close relations overcame any prejudice they might have felt toward his race.

Juárez quietly gained the respect of his neighbors. He never earned much money, but as a lawyer he could afford fancy clothes. Instead he customarily wore a black suit coat and a black hat. This was tasteful attire for a lawyer, but he certainly did not try to impress anyone with his choice of clothing. In fact, there was nothing at all imposing about his outward appearance. Squat and standing only five feet tall he was often called "the little Indian." No one regarded him as handsome. Even his wife said of Juárez, "He is very homely but very good."

Benito Juárez had come to Oaxaca as a frightened and lonely shepherd boy who could barely speak Spanish. In less than thirty years he was one of the city's leading citizens. And his success in Oaxaca was a first step, the first rung on a ladder that would eventually reach the immortal stage in Mexican history that he enjoys today.

FOUR

Governor Juárez

n the 1840s a spirit, called manifest destiny, rose in the United States. This spirit or energy had been simmering for generations, since the Americans first turned westward. Believers in manifest destiny held that it was God's plan for their nation to stretch from the Atlantic to the Pacific, or from sea to sea. No force on earth could stop this divine march west. The powerful senator John C. Calhoun said in 1843, "Our population is rolling toward the shores of the Pacific with an impetus greater than what we realize. It is one of those forward movements which leaves anticipation behind."

Standing in the way of America's westward movement was the independent state of Texas and the rest of Mexico's northern frontier. The almost electric spirit of manifest destiny put the United States and Mexico on the path to war.

After the Alamo and the Battle of San Jacinto, the Americans in Texas claimed they were an independent nation. However

The Northern Frontier and American History Books

Generations of American schoolchildren were taught that their country's history began in 1620, when the Pilgrims established their settlement at Plymouth Rock in Massachusetts. The Pilgrims were said to be the first non-Indian settlers to establish a permanent colony in what became the United States. Those history lessons were inaccurate. More than twenty years before the Pilgrims arrived on the *Mayflower*, Spanish and mestizo colonists came from Mexico and built towns in what they called *Nuevo Mexico* (New Mexico). The present-day city of Santa Fe, New Mexico was founded by Mexican settlers in 1610, ten years before Plymouth Rock. Those long ago Mexicans were, in fact, the first people other than Indians to build permanent settlements in what became the United States.

In the mid-1800s, many Americans believed in manifest destiny, a concept that asserted the divine right of Americans to claim and settle all the land from the Atlantic to the Pacific Oceans. This allegorical painting depicts the American march westward. *(Library of Congress)*

from the beginnings most Texans wanted to become part of the United States. Texas joined the American Union in 1845, when Congress voted to make it the 28th state. Granting statehood to Texas was a violation of principles held sacred in Mexico. To the Mexicans, Texas was a rebellious colony. The government of Mexico refused to recognize Texas as part of the U.S. Friction between the two countries grew and threatened to explode.

In April 1846, President James Polk sent American troops deep into Texas where they camped on the Rio Grande River. This was disputed territory as the border of Texas had always been thought of as the Nueces River, far to the north. Sending soldiers to the Rio Grande was a provocative move on President Polk's part. On April 24, a Mexican army encircled a force

James Polk

Spanish California

California was the most remote region in Mexico's northern frontier. In fact, Mexican government officials looked upon California as an overseas province because it was far easier to reach by sea than by land. By the 1820s, only about 6,000 Mexican settlers lived in California. Los Angeles was a sleepy village and San Francisco was a small port called *Yerba Buena* (Good Herb). Despite its remoteness, Catholic priests from Mexico built a string of twenty-one mission churches along the California coastline. Those missions have been carefully restored and are popular tourist attractions in California today.

The Santa Barbara mission was one of the California missions founded by Spanish priests between 1771 and 1823. *(Library of Congress)*

of sixty-three Americans near the Rio Grande and killed or captured all of them. Claiming American blood has been shed, "upon American soil," President Polk asked congress for a declaration of war on May 11, 1846.

Mexico was woefully unprepared to go to war against its powerful neighbor. It had no stable government in Mexico City. Instead Santa Anna and other opportunists came,

General Zachary Taylor led American troops to many victories in the Spanish-American War. *(Library of Congress)*

proclaimed themselves leaders, and remained in power until their luck ran out. Mexico's army lacked modern weapons, and its soldiers were mostly Indian farmers who were forced into the ranks.

The United States also faced severe challenges in the coming conflict. American soldiers would have to march hundreds of miles over cruel desert lands to reach the interior of Mexico. Looming as an even larger problem was slavery, an issue which was beginning to divide the Americans into two separate and hostile camps. The Mexican War brought this divide into sharper focus. Southerners readily volunteered for the opportunity to fight in Mexico. Many in the

Origin of a Word

The word gringo is a slang word for Americans or other white foreigners that has been used in Mexico for many years. At one time it was thought of as an offensive or even a racist term, but today the word has lost its negative impact. Americans living in Mexico commonly call themselves gringos. Several theories tell of the origin of the term. One theory holds that the word evolved from a song sung by American soldiers on the march in the 1840s. The song, "Green Grow the Lilacs," contained two words "green grow" which when sang together and heard by someone who did not know English sounded like "gringo." Here is the chorus of this popular American marching song which was sung by soldiers in the Mexican War:

Green grow the lilacs, all sparkling with dew;
I'm lonely, my darling, since parting from you.
But by our next meeting I hope to prove true,
And change the green lilacs to the red, white, and blue.

American south wanted to annex all of Mexico and make it one huge slave state. Antislavery northerners viewed the Mexican War as a land seizure which would only benefit the southern states.

President Polk, the primary architect of the war, had no desires to make Mexico an American colony. Polk viewed California as the major prize of the Mexican northern territories. Before the war Polk offered to buy California and New Mexico from the Mexican government, but the Mexicans refused to sell.

On May 18, 1846, American General Zachary Taylor crossed the Rio Grand River with a large army. Before the end of the year Taylor and his forces occupied most of the large cities in northeastern Mexico. The most decisive battle in the northern campaign took place at Buena Vista near the city of Saltillo in February 1847. Here Santa Anna led an army of up to 20,000 men against a force of only 5,000

The War that Made Presidents and Generals

Many American military and political careers began as a result of the Mexican War. General Zachary Taylor used the popularity he gained in the Battle of Buena Vista to win the 1848 election as president of the United States. Other young officers including Grant, Lee, McClellan, Jackson, Pickett, and Meade fought bravely in the Mexican War and became famous generals in the American Civil War (1861-1865). Robert E. Lee led the Confederate forces in the Civil War and Ulysses S. Grant commanded the Union army. Grant, a national hero, was elected President of the United States in 1868 and served two terms.

A depiction of the battle of Buena Vista *(Library of Congress)*

Americans under Taylor's command. Though they were outnumbered four to one the Americans triumphed largely because of their superior artillery.

In March 1847, an army of 10,000 men under the command of General Winfield Scott landed near Veracruz. In twenty days Scott and his men captured the port. The Americans then marched relentlessly towards Mexico City.

General Santa Anna thought of himself as a military genius. His supporters claimed he was "The Napoleon of the West." He made elaborate plans to attack the Americans by using large-scale flanking movements in the classical military style. Tactically he was a competent officer. But when it came to everyday needs such as supplying his armies with food and ammunition, the Napoleon of the West was a failure. Often his men went into combat without proper food or stores of ammunition. The poorly supplied soldiers believed they were beaten even before the battle started, and they deserted in large numbers. Justo Sierra said, "The Mexican soldier proved his good qualities in this frightful carnage. He is a soldier who, when hungry and weary, still fights on with courage and ardor. But . . . when he looses confidence in his officer or his leader he deserts . . . he runs away."

Mexican history books call 1847, the "terrible year" because Mexicans lost battle after battle to the ever advancing Americans. On October 29 of the terrible year, Benito Juárez became governor of Oaxaca. Upon accepting the state governorship Juárez noted his country's perils, "we are called upon to witness the anguish of our country in the terrible moments of her agony." Still the Juárez governorship marked a positive step. He was the first pure-blooded Indian ever to achieve the rank of governor in Mexico.

As governor, Juárez clashed with General Santa Anna. The liberal-conservative feud continued even while Mexico fought for its life against the Americans. In 1847, Santa Anna was in disgrace after losing battles in the field. He decided to move to Oaxaca and plot to recover his popularity. Governor Juárez refused to allow the general to enter his state. Juárez feared that Santa Anna, a leading conservative, would fire up conservative forces and perhaps trigger a civil war in Oaxaca. Santa Anna was enraged at the governor's actions. He blamed the banishment on the long ago incident when Juárez, the college student, waited on his table and the general stared at his bare feet. Santa Anna wrote, "He [Juárez] could not forgive me because he had waited on me at a table in Oaxaca, in December, 1829."

As the American army pressed closer to the capital, the Mexican troops fought bravely. Volunteers poured out of Mexico City to join the ranks of the defenders. But the Mexican forces were poorly equipped and poorly led. In late

Spanish Terms in the American Southwest

In 1848 the Mexican flag was struck in what is now the southwestern states of the U.S. But Spanish place names and terms remained. Seven states—Arizona, California, Colorado, Montana, Nevada, New Mexico, and Texas—all have Spanish names, given to them by Mexican pioneers. This also holds true for many rivers (the Rio Grande for example) and mountain ranges (the Sierra Nevadas). Spanish terms such as arroyo, canyon, and mesa continue to describe the majesty of southwestern land features.

September 1848, the Americans entered Mexico City. Both sides were exhausted.

Hunger reigned and supplies ran thin. The general who led the Americans into the city approached on foot and wore only one boot. A violent street battle broke out in the capital, but ended after only one day. The U.S.-Mexican War was over.

The conflict ended officially with a peace treaty signed February 2, 1848, at the town of Guadalupe Hidalgo near Mexico City. The Treaty of Guadalupe Hidalgo gave the U.S. some 525,000 square miles of what was once Mexico's north-ern frontier. The vast region amounted to more than half the total area of Mexico. This loss of land was made even more costly for Mexico when gold was discovered in California in 1848. The find triggered the great California Gold Rush and made California a prosperous region.

Seeing the Americans—the hated Yankees—take over the northern frontier added to the despair felt by the Mexican people. To a certain extent bitterness caused by the war lingers in Mexico to this day. Writing in 1950, the Mexican philosopher, Octavio Paz, said, "The United States took advantage of [our confused] situation, and in one of the most unjust wars in the history of imperialist expansion, deprived us of over half our territory."

The Mexican defeat was complete. Mexican armies won not a single battle. Yet the soldiers fought with courage and honor. The nation lost because it was not really a modern state. Mexico supported a racial caste system that left Indians with virtually no stake in the government, mestizos with frustrating limited powers, and whites squabbling with each other over the top positions. This racial hierarchy had changed little since the time of New Spain. While many other countries responded to the ideals set down by the Enlightenment, Mexico remained fixed in its almost feudal past.

Benito Juárez was one of many progressive Mexican politicians who recognized his country must change or face collapse. A weakened Mexico could easily be absorbed into the United States or be overwhelmed by a European power. To Juárez, law was the key to Mexico's future. As the Bible contained a set of rules for an individual to follow, a nation's constitution must so bind its citizens. Mexico had no effective constitution, its leaders were often corrupt, and its people had little respect for law. This situation demanded change, and in the years to come Juárez led the forces of change in Mexico.

In 1849, Juárez won a second term as governor of Oaxaca. Normally he was not given to angry speeches, but in his

The Mexican National Anthem

In 1853 the Mexican government announced a contest to write a new national anthem. It was hoped the anthem would inspire Mexican patriotism and offset the sting of defeat in the war against the Americans. The result was the *Himno National Mexicano*. The melody is stirring and the words militant. The National Anthem was first heard in public on September 16, 1854, during that year's Independence Day celebration. Here are the words of the chorus in Spanish and English:

Mexicanos, al grito de guera
el acero aprestad y el brindón,
y retiemble en sus centros la tierra
al sonoro rugir del cañón

Mexicans, at the cry of war,
Prepare the steel and the steed,
And may the earth shake at its center
To the roar of the cannon.

second inaugural address he lashed out at politicians who believed their high rank placed them above the law:

> I am a son of the people and I will not forget it; on the contrary I will stand up for their rights and take care that they learn, that they grow nobler and they create a future for themselves and abandon the path of disorder, vice and misery to which they have been led by men who only in words call themselves friends and liberators but through their actions are the cruelest tyrants.

During his second term, an epidemic of cholera swept through Oaxaca. Guadalupe Juárez, the two-year-old daughter of the

Benito Juárez family, caught the disease and died in 1850. Though they were devastated, Juárez and his wife made burial plans. A recently passed sanitation law required all burials to take place at a municipal cemetery outside of town. The law made exceptions for high-standing politicians such as the governor. Powerful politicians were allowed to bury their loved ones in churchyards as was the custom in the past. Juárez and his wife were serious Catholics and wanted their daughter to be laid to rest on church grounds. But the law which gave him an exception because he was governor was the type of legislation Juárez detested. According to his beliefs, political leaders should not be treated as a privileged class and be guided by a different set of laws. Leading a funeral procession, Benito Juárez carried the tiny coffin of his daughter to the municipal cemetery. He said he acted in this manner, "in order to give an example of obedience to the law." Holding the coffin on his shoulder, he wept all the way to the burial grounds.

Juárez remained governor for four years. The Juárez administration made many accomplishments in Oaxaca. Remembering his own difficulties attending school, he determined his greatest goal was to improve education in the state. As governor he built two to three hundred new schools and eight teacher colleges. Taking a revolutionary step, he insisted these schools be open to girls as well as to boys. Juárez was the first Mexican leader to advocate schooling for females. He once wrote, "To form women with all the requirements of their necessary and elevated mission is to form the fertile seed of regeneration, of social betterment. For this reason, their education should never be neglected."

During his governorship he sent farm experts to the fields to teach crop rotation and the latest agricultural techniques. When government offices opened at nine o'clock in the morning he was at his desk, and he insisted every minor officeholder report to his job on time and not take days off. Juárez regularly took attendance at nine A.M., and he was not afraid to reprehend other officeholders who were tardy or chronically absent. Governor Juárez built roads and bridges. He collected taxes, did not waste the state's money, and paid the government's bills. The governor took over a state that was deeply in debt and left it financially sound.

In 1852, Juárez retired as governor. He had served two terms and believed he had accomplished his mission to set Oaxaca on a progressive course. He was forty-six years old and wanted to spend more time with his growing family. Juárez returned to the Institute of Science and Arts, a school he loved. He was named the school's director and he taught his favorite course—law. This was a splendid time for the Juárez family. He was a respected college professor and a practicing attorney. Perhaps, if left alone, he would remain in the college environment for life.

But internal upheavals still shook Mexico. In March 1853, Juárez sat on the balcony of his house quietly talking to his wife. Suddenly a man standing on the street below drew a pistol and fired at him. The bullet missed. Though the shooter wore a disguise, Juárez knew he was Máximo Ortiz, a neighbor and once a fellow member of the liberal party. Now Ortiz was an enemy. Juárez pounded on Ortiz's door, but his wife insisted the man was not home. Juárez suspected Ortiz was hiding inside. The shooting incident opened a new chapter in Juárez's life. Because of his country's internal warfare, he became a hunted man.

In Mexico City, Antonio López de Santa Anna had taken control of the government once more. Santa Anna and the conservatives were determined to punish all their enemies from the liberal faction—including Benito Juárez. It is not known if the shooter, Máximo Ortiz, acted under orders from leading conservatives or if the assassination attempt was just part of the bitter party politics of the time.

Two months after the shooting event Juárez was arrested by federal troops acting under the orders of Santa Anna and was taken on horseback to the state of Veracruz. He was not allowed to say goodbye to his wife and children. For weeks Juárez was held in an ancient prison near the port

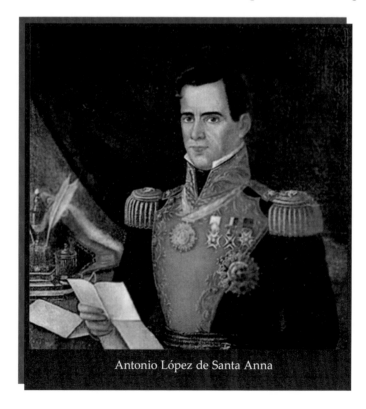

Antonio López de Santa Anna

of Veracruz. Without the benefit of a trial, Juárez was banished from Mexico by authorities loyal to Santa Anna. He took a boat to Cuba and eventually sailed to New Orleans. Juárez knew New Orleans held a small community of exiled Mexicans who were members of the liberal party. His wife, needing to earn money, opened a small store where she sold cloth and candy in order to support the family. Both she and her husband were heartbroken at the forced separation.

With Juárez and other leading liberals in jail or in exile, Santa Anna entrenched his power over Mexico. He now preferred to be called "Prince President" or "His Most Serene Royal Highness."

Juárez was hundreds of miles away from his family and his country. He plotted ways to return home and he never lost his faith in the purity of law. Always he recalled the speech he made when taking over the office of governor of Oaxaca, "We have a fundamental charter in which are stated the rights and duties of the governors and the governed. This charter, then, will be my only guide, and its strict observance and the execution of the laws that come from the legitimate representatives of the people will merit my exclusive dedication."

FIVE

Juárez and the Reform

J uárez arrived in New Orleans in 1854, and took residence in a shabby hotel called the Cincinnati. He had no money. With several other Mexicans, he rolled cigars and cigarettes during the day and sold them on the streets in the evenings. In this manner he earned enough to buy black bread and coffee and to pay his meager rent. The only luxury he allowed himself was to occasionally buy a used book.

This was Juárez' first visit to the United States and he was both fascinated and shocked by his new surroundings. The country's riches impressed him. While many New Orleans residents lived in poverty, the city markets held a wealth of goods and most people worked for a living. Everywhere crews built new houses and stores. Juárez attributed this lively business environment to the fact that Americans allowed free trade between their states. Mexico, on the other hand, restricted or taxed goods moving from one state to another. Free trade, he concluded, was a goal Mexico should work towards.

In 1854, Juárez was exiled to New Orleans by order of Santa Anna.
(Library of Congress)

One aspect of American life horrified him: Slavery was legal and widespread in the state of Louisiana where he lived. He wondered how the Americans, so progressive in most matters, could allow the vile practice of slavery in their country. All around him he saw slaves, some of whom were bound in chains. Men and women were bought and sold in New Orleans slave markets as if they were cattle. His friends said Juárez became particularly upset when he saw slave women working in the fields under the watchful eyes of masters who could have them whipped if their work was in anyway improper.

The inhumanity of slavery was imposed on the people because of the color of their skin. Even free blacks were treated as if they were criminals. At eight o'clock each evening a sheriff stood in downtown New Orleans and fired his rifle

During his time in New Orleans, Juárez was appalled by the cruel treatment of slaves in America. *(Library of Congress)*

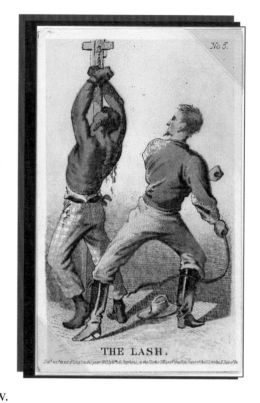

THE LASH.

into the air. The gunshot meant all people of color—including free blacks—must be off the streets or face arrest. The Indian Juárez, whose skin color was as dark as many of the African Americans, had to abide by this curfew.

The exiled Mexicans, most of whom were followers of the liberal party, formed a close group in New Orleans. One banished Mexican liberal was Melchor Ocampo. Although they became close friends, Juárez and Ocampo had opposite backgrounds. Ocampo was born into wealth and attended the best schools. As a young man he traveled to Europe where he studied languages, philosophy, art, and science. Ocampo fell under the influence of the French writers Rousseau and Voltaire who advocated equality for every member of a society. In his home state of Michoacán, Ocampo entered politics and rose to the rank of governor. In office, Ocampo fought for the rights of poor and landless people. Like Juárez, he offended Santa Anna and was exiled.

In New Orleans, Juárez became close friends with fellow liberal exile Melchor Ocampo. *(Library of Congress)*

On the issue of religion, Ocampo and Juárez represented two divergent views. Ocampo, the student of philosophy, saw no need for a belief in God. To Juárez, the stoic Indian, belief in God was fundamental. Yet both men felt the Catholic Church held too much political power in Mexico. They wished to see their country move towards a separation of church and state along the lines of the United States.

Melchor Ocampo was the most famous of the Mexican liberals who had been forced to leave the country. Many politicians predicted Ocampo would some day win the presidency under the liberal banner. Juárez, on the other hand, was a rather obscure ex-governor and was little known outside of his state. At the time of their exile, Ocampo was forty-two years old and Juárez was forty-eight. Once one of Mexico's richest men, Ocampo made a meager living in New Orleans by selling pots and pans door-to-door.

Juárez' spirits were low while living in New Orleans. He missed his family and he grieved for his country. On one occasion Ocampo worried when he did not see his friend all day. Ocampo feared Juárez had fallen victim to the city's waterfront thugs who beat and robbed foreigners. He later discovered Juárez had spent the entire day at the pier checking arriving boats, hoping to get a letter from his wife. The coveted letter never came.

In Mexico, Santa Anna's government weakened. Santa Anna had received $10 million dollars from the United States for a land sale called the Gadsden Purchase. The money was supposed to be spent funding schools and other government services, but instead it went to expand the army. Among other things Santa Anna used American dollars to buy glittering new uniforms for his palace guards. When the money ran out, top army officers deserted the Santa Anna cause.

In the port city of Acapulco, a rebellion began against Santa Anna. The uprising was led by an aging military man named Juan Alvarez. General Alvarez had been an officer in Mexico's War of Independence, and for decades supported the liberals. Alvarez, an Indian, teamed with a white liberal politician named Ignacio Commonfort and published the Plan

The Gadsden Purchase

The treaty which ended the Mexican War in 1848 was unclear as to the exact boarder line between the two countries in the region of what are now the states of New Mexico and Arizona. The Gadsden Purchase, signed on December 30, 1853, gave the disputed region (29,640 square miles) to the U.S. The treaty was negotiated by James Gadsden, the U.S. minister to Mexico. It was the final step in establishing the U.S./Mexican border as it is today.

of Ayutla in March 1854. The three-step plan called for the overthrow of Santa Anna, then the establishment of a temporary government, and finally the writing of a constitution.

The Plan of Ayutla infuriated Santa Anna. Leading a large army he marched into the state of Guerrero (where Acapulco

Liberal general Juan Alvarez initiated a plan to overthrow the conservative government of Santa Anna.

is located), determined to crush the movement. However in the Guerrero Mountains and jungles the wily warrior Alvarez was invincible. Santa Anna burned some Indian villages and executed many liberal politicians, but he could not quash the rebellion.

In New Orleans, Juárez read about the Plan of Ayutla and the uprising in Guerrero. He determined this was a movement

Ignacio Commonfort became the first liberal president of Mexico. His presidency ushered a period of social reform known as La Reforma.

he must join. Ultimately the Plan of Ayutla would lead to a constitution for Mexico. Juárez, a man of law, believed a constitution was essential to bring peace and order to his country.

In September 1855, Juárez left New Orleans on a ship bound for Panama. He crossed the Isthmus of Panama on land. Once on the Pacific side he boarded another ship headed north toward Acapulco. The California Gold Rush was in its full frenzy at the time. His fellow passengers included many American gold seekers eagerly sailing to San Francisco while dreaming of California riches.

In Acapulco, Juárez walked miles over a country road to reach Alvarez' headquarters. A sudden rainstorm struck and ruined his only set of clothes. A kindly soldier gave him cotton trousers and a shirt. Juárez was greeted at the camp by an officer who happened to be Alvarez' son. The younger Alvarez was startled when Juárez asked if there was any mail for him. With his plain cotton clothes, this man looked like a simple middle-aged Indian soldier who probably could not read. Then the man announced he was Benito Juárez, the one-time governor of Oaxaca. Alvarez asked why he did not introduce himself as an important person when he first reported to camp. Juárez said, "Because, what importance has that?"

Santa Anna, meanwhile, realized he could not defeat his liberal enemies who were growing stronger in Guerrero. In August 1855, he slipped out of Mexico City taking with him as much gold as he could loot from the nation's treasury. His foes in the capital celebrated by breaking up the expensive coaches the president used on inspection tours and making a bonfire of the pieces.

With his exit in 1855, the Age of Santa Anna came to a close. For thirty years Santa Anna had dominated Mexico. His off-and-on again leadership almost led to the country's ruin. He lived another twenty years, mostly on a huge farm he owned in Venezuela. Often Santa Anna lost money on investment schemes. In 1872, he was allowed to return to Mexico. Santa Anna died in Mexico City in 1876, friendless and in poverty.

On November 14, 1855, Alvarez rode into Mexico City with an army of Indian warriors. The fickle Mexico City crowd, who months earlier cheered Santa Anna, now welcomed their new leader as if he were a savior. One of Alvarez' first acts was to appoint Benito Juárez, a legal scholar, as his minister of justice. Melchor Ocampo was named a minister on the cabinet and served as intellectual leader of the new government.

Alvarez was well in his seventies. He could barely read, and knew he would not function well as a political leader. Therefore, he surrendered his authority to fellow liberal Ignacio Commonfort. So far the Plan of Ayutla was being followed to its letter. Commonfort was to head a temporary government until a constitution could be written. When a new constitution was in place, the Plan of Ayutla would be complete. From the beginning Juárez approved of the Plan, once calling it, "the memorable Plan of Ayutla which offers a remedy to a great wrong."

Commonfort began a movement called *La Reforma* (The Reform). The Reform started as an extension of the contest between liberals and conservatives, but grew into a religious and racial war. Liberal forces wanted to curb the power of the Catholic Church. Catholic leaders took their people to war rather than accept any limitations on the powers they enjoyed. The Reform movement was led largely by mestizos. By the 1850s, mestizos had become the largest race in Mexico. An ambitious people, the mestizos would no longer accept a position behind the whites.

Intellectually the Reform was grounded in the French Revolution (1789–1799). Mexicans had long been influenced by French thought. During the French Revolution impoverished and landless peasant farmers took over their government and imposed new laws redistributing land and wealth. The result of the French Revolution was a strong peasantry. Melchor Ocampo hoped to see a similar outcome in Mexico. Though Ocampo was himself a wealthy landowner, he wanted to

La Raza

Mexican census takers stopped recording racial categories in 1920, so it is impossible to give exact figures as to the country's racial makeup today. Experts agree mestizos are the majority, far outnumbering Indians and whites. Mexico also has a small black population.

Mestizos are called La Raza (the race). Columbus Day, October 12, is known as *Dia de La Raza* (Day of the Race), and it is a national holiday in Mexico. People celebrate because Columbus' voyage led to the mixing of Spanish and Indian bloodlines and thus the creation of the new race. A statue of Columbus stands in most Mexican towns, and on Columbus Day schoolchildren decorate the statue with flowers.

Interestingly, Columbus never set foot on Mexican soil. The Spaniard Hernan Cortés had far more to do with the creation of the Mexican mestizos. But Mexican historians condemn Cortés as a cruel conqueror and nowhere in the country will one find his statue.

break up the country's rich estates and turn Mexico into a land of small farmers.

The Mexican Reform and the French Revolution had many other parallels. Both ushered in periods of civil strife in their respective countries. Both movements led to the rise of dictators. The French Revolution and the Mexican reform promised greater freedom and prosperity to the lower classes. However the land redistribution envisioned by Ocampo never developed. Mexico remained a country of a few large land-owners and many landless peasants. The Reform was more a clash of ideas rather than a contest between personalities. In the past Mexicans fought for the glory of individuals such as Santa Anna. Now they would fight for principals such as establishing freedom of religion in their country. This development alone proved Mexico was becoming a modern state. As the philosopher Octavio Paz said, "Mexico was born during the epoch of the Reform. She was conceived, invented, projected in it and through it."

As minister of justice in the new government, Juárez wrote an important law which came to be called *Ley Juárez* (the Juárez Law). This law abolished fueros (powers) long held by the military and the clergy. In the past, if a military man broke the law, he could be tried only by a military court. Clergymen also enjoyed the privilege of being judged only by tribunals made up of fellow priests. Neither soldiers nor priests had to face civil courts as did ordinary Mexicans. To Juárez the old system of special courts was a damnable example of privileged classes operating in Mexican society. He believed the law ought to be applied equally to all citizens.

The controversial Juárez law was joined by another new act called Ley Lerdo. Written by head of the treasury, Miguel Lerdo de Tejada, *Ley Lerdo* cut into the church's vast property holdings. At the time the Catholic Church of Mexico owned more than one third of the country's total land. Powerful priests lived on haciendas (ranches) which covered thousands of acres. Provisions in the Lerdo Law required the church to sell all its land except for the ground underneath the church buildings. The Mexican government was to collect taxes on the sales. Thus Ley Lerdo would provide revenue for the government as well as promote small farm ownership, the dream of Ocampo. Acts similar to *Ley Juárez* and *Ley Lerdo* had helped to reform French society and elevate the status of the peasants.

Mexican priests and military officers denounced the two new laws written by the liberals. Priests gave parishioners banners which read "Long Live Religion" and led them on marches to government buildings. High-ranking bishops threatened to excommunicate (expel from the church) all liberals who supported the new laws.

Through most of 1856, the country waited breathlessly as people expected a war to break out between the liberal and conservative sides. Liberals feared their enemies were secretly stashing weapons inside churches. With that suspicion in mind, Commonfort ordered the destruction of the Convent of San Francisco, a revered Mexico City church erected three hundred years earlier by Spaniards. A crew of four hundred workers approached the old church, but stopped when priests warned that anyone damaging the structure would be punished by hellfire. Finally a liberal politician grabbed a pick and delivered the first blows to the church walls. The others followed and the church was razed. The destruction of the church was one of the first episodes of a bloody chapter in Mexican history called the War of the Reform.

Despite the strife in the capital, a convention composed of lawyers and political leaders met in 1856 to write a new constitution. Religion was the most inflammatory issue debated at the constitutional convention. Many liberals wanted freedom of religion written into the new set of laws. Conservatives and even a large percentage of liberals insisted Catholicism should remain a national religion. Fighting words such as "bloodsucking priests" were cried out by the anti-church faction while the pro-Catholics charged their foes were "vile sinners." Finally the constitution was written in such a way that it contained no specific language endorsing Catholicism,

Juárez holding the 1857 Mexican constitution

nor did it have wording allowing for religious freedom. This compromise satisfied no one and the explosive question of religion lingered.

The constitution was ratified in February 1857. Juárez, who was respected as a legal scholar, helped write the new document. Although the wording was loose regarding religion, the constitution did endorse Ley Juárez and Ley Lerdo. This meant the Constitution of 1857 enraged the clergy and the military. The government decreed all officeholders were required to swear allegiance to the constitution. The church countered by claiming anyone taking the oath would face excommunication.

Abiding by the constitution, elections were held in 1857. Commonfort won the presidency and Benito Juárez was elected as president of the Supreme Court. This post was significant as Mexico had no vice president. Under the law, the president of the Supreme Court was next in line to take over the office of president in the event of a vacancy.

Juárez divided his time between Mexico City and Oaxaca. He was happiest at home when he was with his family and surrounded by his children. Juárez and his wife Margarita were devoted to each other. Affectionately he called her his "old lady," even though he was twenty years older than Margarita. In all they had twelve children: six daughters and six sons. Because death came with cruel frequency to the young in those days, three of the girls died as babies.

The instability caused by the Reform made Juárez always cast an eye toward the capital. Mexico finally had a constitution which he hoped would guide the nation to a new era of peace under the law. He did not agree with all the clauses in the Constitution of 1857. Still a great deal of work, sacrifice, and compromise had gone into the creation of the 1857 document. He once called the new constitution the "precious fruit the people have gathered . . . in order to gain their liberties." Along with hundreds of other public officials, he swore an oath to the Constitution. He would fight for the set of laws and if necessary he would die for the Constitution of Mexico.

SIX

A Besieged Presidency

President Ignacio Commonfort abhorred violence. Like Juárez he was devoted to the law and he hoped the Constitution of 1857 would bring peace and order to Mexico. But the document required the church to surrender its excess lands. The constitution also made priests and military officers give up their special privileges—the jealously guarded *fueros*. Instead of abiding by the Constitution, the priests aligned with the military and raised a battle cry: *religión y fueros* (religion and powers). Tension between those backing the new constitution and those loyal to the church and the military resulted in the War of the Reform, also called the Three Years War. It was a bloody but significant period in Mexican history. Despite the blood spilled in the war, Mexico advanced to become a new country.

Paseo de La Reforma

The Reform movement and the War of the Reform is such a powerful era in Mexican history that most towns today have a boulevard or major road named *La Reforma* as a tribute to that time. The grandest of these is Paseo de la Reforma in Mexico City, a treelined boulevard which cuts through the heart of the capital. The boulevard (often simply called "The Paseo" or "The Reforma") holds Mexico City's most elegant high rise buildings.

The War of the Reform began in 1857, shortly after the new constitution was ratified. There was no dramatic spark that launched the fighting. The reform movement graduated from a war of words between liberals and conservatives into a shooting war. The clash displayed all the cruelties of a war based upon religion. Priests convinced soldiers that God was on their side and therefore they could commit no sins in the course of their holy battles. According to the clergy God condoned the shooting or the torturing of prisoners. The priests said that such atrocities, done under the banner of *religión y fueros*, were pardoned and even blessed by the Lord.

The War of the Reform was fought with shocking violence and cruelty. Justo Sierra said, "The abominable custom of shooting captive officers prevailed since the struggle began." Not only officers but soldiers and civilians were slaughtered by troops of both sides. Sierra adds that after one typical battle, "for good measure the doctors of the vanquished army and a number of peasants were ruthlessly shot."

Near the close of 1857, a general named Félix Zuloaga ousted Commonfort from office and seized power. One of Zuloaga's first acts was to arrest Benito Juárez and hold him prisoner. Days later Commonfort arranged for Juárez to be released from custody. In January 1858, Commonfort, a sad and broken man, left Mexico for exile in New York.

The constitution was clear that in the event of the president's absence the next person in line of succession was the president of the Supreme Court. This was the position held by Juárez. Fifty-one-year old Benito Juárez was now the president of Mexico, even though Zuloaga actually headed the government in Mexico City. Amazingly, the new president was a full-blooded Zapotec Indian, born in poverty, who grew up a shepherd. For the first time in its 340-year history, Mexico had an Indian president.

But Juárez inherited a nation consumed by disorder and war. Most Mexicans, confused by the fast-moving events, could not tell who their president was. In the capital Zuloaga, the man claiming to be president, was already fighting off conservative rivals who sought the seat of power. The countryside was alive with tension as generals chose sides between liberals and conservatives. Priests in churches melted down their crosses and statues in order to collect gold and buy guns. In scattered towns, pitched battles raged.

Although Juárez was the constitutional president, he was not safe in Mexico City. He and a few advisors fled, seeking a haven where they could establish a base and set up a rival government. They slept in fields as they traveled. Kindly farmers gave the men meals of tortillas and beans. This hungry and homeless band made up the early presidential staff of Benito Juárez.

One of the men fleeing with Juárez was a poet turned politician named Guillermo Prieto. Born in Mexico City, Prieto was a biting writer of satire. In the past he made

As Juárez fled Mexico City, he was accompanied by Guillermo Prieto (above)

sport of Antonio López de Santa Anna and was jailed several times because of his writings. One subject he particularly enjoyed covering in essays was Santa Anna's love for riding in fancy coaches with gold gilding. While traveling with Juárez his group once rode in a coach draped with black robes. The robes made the coach look like a funeral carriage and because of the disguise enemy troops allowed it to pass through their ranks.

In the city of Guadalajara, Juárez and his companions were seized by soldiers who hours earlier claimed they were sympathetic to the liberal side. Loyalties shifted faster than the wind during the War of the Reform. While he was held prisoner, soldiers loyal to Juárez attacked Guadalajara. The attack infuriated the local commander, and Juárez suddenly found himself facing a firing squad. As Juárez stood with his back to a wall an officer with a raised sword commanded his riflemen: "Ready . . . aim . . ." Juárez looked at the soldiers with an almost serene gaze, as if it did not matter if they shot him. At the command of "aim," the poet Prieto jumped in front of his president and shouted to the soldiers, "Put up your arms! Put up your arms! Brave men are not assassins." The soldiers, stunned by the acts of bravery from both Juárez and Prieto, withdrew their rifles. After seeing Juárez stand so steadfast even in the face of death, the poet Prieto wrote, "my heart broke out in a tempest of tears."

It was during the chaotic War of the Reform that Juárez began to win the respect of his country's citizens. The quiet man many called "the little Indian" stood for law. His nation had a constitution which said he was the president. The constitution was the highest law of the land. Now, despite the powerful forces which opposed him, he boldly defended the spirit of that law. His faith in law was as strong as his religious beliefs. He once said, "to carry out the law has always been my sword and shield."

With enemy armies pursuing him Juárez retreated to the port city of Veracruz, a liberal stronghold. The city was protected by soldiers loyal to the man who they believed was their president. Also Veracruz was the country's principal port on the Atlantic. Holding the port allowed Juárez and the liberals to collect taxes from incoming ships. With tax money the liberals supported an army and bought weapons.

A famous story is told about racial standards prevailing in Veracruz when Juárez arrived. Veracruz had long held a large community of blacks who were brought there generations earlier as slaves of the Spaniards. As time passed, the blacks advanced in the social order to the point where they were above Indians. When the president and his staff rented rooms at an inn, Juárez asked a black maid to fetch him a bucket of water so he could wash his hands and face. The maid noted that he was an Indian and reasoned he was a servant of the president. She gruffly told him to fetch the water himself. This Juárez did without a word of complaint. The next morning the maid saw Juárez seated at the head of a conference table issuing orders to his ministers who were white and mestizo. The black woman hastily made the Sign of the Cross and raced out of town. She feared she would be punished for insulting the President of Mexico who—shockingly—was an Indian.

All rules and courtesies were abandoned during the War of Reform. In previous Mexican civil wars a political leader's wife and children were regarded as neutrals and spared deliberate harm. But this was a religious war. With God on their side, army officers were free from sin and allowed to capture and even kill women and children.

In Oaxaca, Margarita Juárez heard rumors that the conservatives planned to kidnap her and her children. She set out on a journey of more than two hundred miles over mountains and through rain forests to reach her husband in Veracruz. Margarita never wrote about the details of her escape, but it must have been a harrowing trek on foot for her and her family. At the time she had eight children, ranging in age from a baby to a fourteen-year-old. Shunning main roads in favor of mountain trails, the journey took more than a month. Throughout the walk she was guarded by Zapotec volunteer soldiers who were determined to fight to the death to protect the family of Benito Juárez.

Juárez accepted his role as a wartime president, but dreamed of how much more he could accomplish if Mexico were at peace. One of his dreams was to build a school system and make education free and mandatory for every Mexican child. He also made plans to bring his own people—the Indians—into full citizenship. Although a few individuals were able to rise in status, most Mexican Indians endured backward lives in segregated enclaves. An observer writing in 1857 said, "The Indians are spread throughout the entire territory of the republic, grouped in small communities and forming really a family apart from the white and mixed races . . . [they have never] been taught anything more than to fear God, the priest, and the mayor."

Land reform was the dream of Melchor Ocampo. In those areas controlled by the liberals, Ocampo enforced laws which broke up the large estates owned by individuals and the church and distributed the land to the poor. Ocampo hoped to make Mexico a nation of independent farmers similar to agrarian society in the United States. However the Indians did not know how to do the paperwork involved in government land sales, and priests told mestizos that buying land confiscated from the church was a sin. Because of these difficulties Mexico remained a nation of a few large landowners and great masses of landless peasants.

The majority of Mexicans favored the liberals, but the conservatives had money provided by the church and skilled officers from the army. Miguel Miramón, though only in his twenties, was one of Mexico's most successful generals. Leading his conservative troops Miramón conquered the

General Miguel Miramón *(Library of Congress)*

northern city of San Luis Potsi and then marched on cities along the Pacific coast. He was famed and feared for killing captives and burning villages which harbored resistors. Another conservative general, Tomás Mejía, was an Indian who displayed the same toughness and courage as did Juárez. General Mejía believed the conservatives were fighting on the side of God and righteousness.

General Tomás Mejía believed God favored a conservative government that supported a strong Catholic presence in Mexico. *(Library of Congress)*

The War of the Reform was largely a guerilla war, fought without definitive battle lines. While conservative forces captured cities, much of the countryside remained in the hands of their liberal enemies. Bands of liberals attacked conservative supply columns on roadsides, killing troops and capturing supplies and horses. Even the best conservative army officers were unable to halt these hit-and-run raids.

Juárez and the liberals had an aggressive general of their own in a young man named Porfirio Díaz. A Mixtec Indian from Oaxaca, Díaz was once a law student and attended Professor Benito Juárez' classes. But young Porfirio Díaz was more attracted to horseback riding than he was to studying law books. As an army officer he was cunning and coura-geous. Díaz won battles for the liberal forces and suffered many wounds while leading his men.

Adding to the confusion of the time was a split in conser-vative ranks. In December of 1858 General Miramón ousted Zuloaga and declared himself president of Mexico. Zuloaga escaped to a stronghold in the city of Puebla and claimed he was still president. So now three men—the conservatives Miramón and Zuloaga and the liberal Juárez—all insisted they were president of the republic.

The chaotic situation encouraged foreign powers to pon-der taking over Mexico. The Mexican government owed large sums of money to banks in England, Spain, and France. Representatives of these countries threatened to seize Mexican ports and collect taxes to pay off the debts. Even some Mexicans reluctantly agreed that a foreign takeover was the best way to stop the civil war and bring the nation to some degree of order. The conservative leader Miramón approached the French with plans to bring European officials to Mexico to act as a new government.

The United States vigorously opposed any European moves on its southern neighbor. In 1823 the United States issued the Monroe Doctrine, named after President James Monroe. The Monroe Doctrine warned European countries not to interfere in the internal affairs of any country in the Western Hemisphere. The Americans feared a European colony taking root in the Western Hemisphere could be used as a base for an attack on U.S. territory.

In the War of the Reform the United States backed Juárez and the liberals. Leaders in Washington concluded the liberals were less likely to work with Europeans bent on establishing

interests in Mexico. The United States sent money and supplies to Juárez in Veracruz. The U.S navy captured several
Spanish ships which were attempting to lay siege to Veracruz.
Munitions from the United States flowed into Veracruz and
bolstered the liberal army.

The Tehuantepec Canal

Another reason the United States favored the liberals during
the War of the Reform was because Juárez was willing to cooperate
with American plans to build a shipping right-of-way through
southern Mexico.

In the late 1850s, leaders in Washington wanted to construct
an American-owned railroad or a canal through a narrow part of
southern Mexico called Tehuantepec. Juárez reasoned that selling
Tehuantepec land to the U.S. would bring much needed revenue
to the Mexican treasury, however the sale would also amount to
a surrender of Mexican territory to the Yankees. Even Justo Sierra,
an admirer of Juárez, said, "That such a pact [the Tehuantepec
land sale] should have appeared feasible to men of such patriotic
mettle as Juárez and Ocampo is shocking."

The completion of the American transcontinental railroad
(1869) and the Panama Canal (1914) negated America's need for a
right-of-way through Mexico and the proposed Tehuantepec sale
is now a footnote in history.

The liberal forces were made up mainly of uneducated
mestizos as soldiers and idealistic white lawyers and teachers as officers. In early battles this amateur army was routed
by the professional and experienced fighting men employed
by the conservatives. At one point the conservative forces
pressed so close to Veracruz that their artillery screamed

through the streets. But slowly the liberals gained strength. In August of 1860, a liberal army won a major victory at the city of Silao, and captured 2,000 enemy soldiers. In what was then a magnificent display of civility, the liberals released their war prisoners unharmed.

In the countryside, Juárez's reputation grew in stature because of his stubborn resistance. He was the constitutional president of Mexico and he would let no enemy take his rightful office. Mexicans, especially the poor and the disposed, learned to love this little man who displayed such bravery. When he left his headquarters in Veracruz, he traveled in a plain black stagecoach and always wore a simple black hat. The clothes and coach, similar to those used by any small businessman, became symbols of his leadership.

In late 1860s, the conservatives were defeated in a series of battles and knew they had lost the War of the Reform.

Juárez's plain black stagecoach symbolized his commitment to the common people of Mexico.

Conservative leader Miguel Miramón fled the capital and made his way to Jalapa, where he was picked up by a French ship. Mexicans would soon see more of Miguel Miramón, the brilliant but ruthless army general. Zuloaga, who still claimed to be president, escaped to Cuba where he retired from politics and entered the tobacco business.

The War of the Reform or the Three Years War lasted from 1858 through 1860. A civil war, it was savage, brutal, and hate filled. The war was also the bloodiest conflict so far in Mexican history. More than 50,000 Mexicans—the true casualty figure will never be known—died during the fighting. However the war gave birth to the modern state of Mexico. Because of the war, the church lost its vast landholdings and the old white ruling class lost its hold on government. Mestizos, the nation's majority race, assumed high political offices. As the philosopher Octavio Paz wrote, "The reform movement founded Mexico and denied the past. It rejected tradition and sought to justify itself in the future."

On January 11, 1861, Juárez and his black carriage arrived in Mexico City. The War of the Reform was now formally over, even though bitter feelings simmered between liberals and conservatives. Only a small crowd greeted the constitutional president. Juárez was a hero to the country people, but he was little known in the capital. Despite the absence of fanfare, this was a historical moment because Mexico was now ruled by a constitutional leader. Juárez had fought a war in defense of a constitution and he was determined to govern according to the terms of that document. He wrote a slogan for the policies he would pursue in the future of his presidency: "Nothing by force, everything through law and reason."

SEVEN

The French Intervention

O n April 12, 1861, Southern artillery fired on Fort Sumter in the American state of South Carolina, plunging America into its terrible civil war. On the surface it would seem the conflict in the United States should have little consequence for Mexicans. But history proves great events in one nation often have a rippling effect and trigger events in another. The American Civil War made possible a foreign invasion of Mexico. The roots of that invasion took hold decades earlier in France.

Of the political and philosophical stirrings sweeping the world in the late eighteenth century, none had the passion of the French Revolution. The Revolution began when educated French people questioned the ancient notion that kings ruled by divine rights—as if they acted under orders issued by God. In 1789 French peasants seized power from their king while chanting: *"Liberté, Égalité, Fraternité!"* ("Liberty, Equality, Fraternity!"). The French Revolution then evolved into its own

The American Civil War made it impossible for America to prevent a French invasion of Mexico. *(Library of Congress)*

form of dictatorship and later became a conquering military force under General Napoleon Bonaparte.

By the 1860s the French Revolution was a memory, but its ideals still gripped the world. Also another Napoleon—Napoleon III—ruled France. The nephew of the famous Bonaparte, Napoleon III became emperor of France in 1852. He sought to build an empire and restore France to its old glory. Mexico, an unstable country at war with itself, loomed as a prize in the empire Napoleon envisioned.

To Napoleon, all the elements needed to seize Mexico began to fall neatly into place. The United States was locked in a brutal civil war. While the Americans fought each other,

Napoleon III *(Library of Congress)*

Washington could not invoke the Monroe Doctrine and send military forces to oust a French army in Mexico. During the War of the Reform the government of Mexico borrowed heavily from European banks. Unpaid debts provided a ready excuse for a European takeover. Also Mexico had natural resources which would benefit a new French empire in the Americas. Mexican fields grew rich harvests of coffee and sugarcane, items in constant demand in Europe. Mexican mines produced one-third of the silver then circulating in the world.

Finally, Napoleon argued, the Mexicans themselves cried out for new leadership: a history of constant military upheavals stood as proof the Mexican people were unable to govern themselves. They needed the firm but loving hand of a king or an emperor to guide them into a bright future. Thus the spirit of the French Revolution took an ironic reversal in thought: The ancient beliefs were correct; kings, not the people, were the proper leaders of a society.

A new Mexican congress narrowly reelected Juárez as president in 1861. Juárez presided over a nation still torn by the War of the Reform. The conservative leader Miramón plotted with the French. The Indian general Tomás Mejía, who believed God sided with the conservatives, established a stronghold in the city of Querétaro.

Hoping to soothe the tempers left by the war, Juárez issued an amnesty order. The order forgave all conservative politicians and military men for their past actions and invited them to join Mexican society as full citizens. The amnesty infuriated Melchor Ocampo, who believed the conservatives should be punished. In protest, Ocampo resigned from Juárez cabinet. In May 1861, a detachment of one-time conservative soldiers pounded on Ocampo's door and carried him off. After riding for three days the soldiers stood Ocampo against a tree and shot him. Juárez had lost a friend who dated back to his time of exile in New Orleans. The murder proved that Mexico was still a land where disputes were settled with bloodshed.

Juárez struggled to pay Mexico's staggering debts. Previous governments borrowed from foreigners, often at outrageous interest rates. Now war torn Mexico produced little revenue while demands for repayment intensified. In July 1861, President Juárez announced a two-year moratorium on paying Mexico's foreign debts. He did not ask the foreign banks to forgive the debts; he simply claimed he needed more time to pay.

In early 1862, naval forces from Great Britain, Spain, and France took over Veracruz in a move to compel Mexico to repay its loans. Washington feared a European kingdom would emerge on its doorstep, and President Abraham Lincoln issued a stern warning: "A foreign monarchy set up on Mexican soil . . . would be an insult to the republican form of government which is most widely spread on the American continent, and would mean the beginning rather than the end of revolution in Mexico." However the United States was powerless to take military action because the American Civil War raged in its full fury.

Negotiations soon satisfied the demands of the Spanish and the British and their navys sailed away from Mexican shores. The forces of France remained. Despite his name and the memory of his illustrious uncle, Napoleon III was not a popular leader. Now he saw his chance to dazzle the French people by building an empire in the Americas. Using unpaid debts as a pretext, the French Emperor ordered his armies to march on Mexico City.

French commanders believed the Mexicans stood no chance against their forces who were thought to be the finest soldiers in the world at the time. Officers of the French army were schooled in military academies established fifty years earlier by the brilliant Napoleon

Bonaparte, one of the most gifted generals in world history. In April 1862, the French general, Comte de Lorencez, wrote to Napoleon in Paris, "We are so superior to the Mexicans in race, organization, morality, and elevated sentiments that I [wish to] inform the Emperor that at the head of six thousand soldiers I am already master of Mexico."

In May 1862, General Lorencez and his men approached the city of Puebla, about one hundred miles from the capital.

Ignacio Zaragoza commanded the small Mexican force at Puebla, which repelled highly trained and heavily armed French troops on May 5th, 1862. *(Library of Congress)*

Defending Puebla was a force of some 6,000 Mexican soldiers, most of whom manned two forts. The Mexicans were commanded by Ignacio Zaragoza. He was a pudgy man who wore glasses and looked more like a school teacher than a military officer. Mexican soldiers were armed with fifty-year-old rifles which were bought from the British and last used to fight Napoleon Bonaparte in the 1815 Battle of Waterloo. Many Indian troops had no rifles at all and fought only with machetes. Artillery pieces in the forts were ninety years old. Still, Ignacio Zaragoza inspired his men. Before the battle he proclaimed, "Your enemies are the first soldiers in the world, but you are the first sons of Mexico. They have come to take your country from you."

On May 5, 1862, a vastly overconfident General Lorencez led his troops to Fort Guadalupe outside of Puebla. First the general ordered his artillerymen to bombard the building. After just a few volleys he signaled the infantry to charge. Lorencez did not want to waste ammunition with a long artillery barrage. He was certain the Mexican defenders would surrender or flee at the first sight of French bayonets. As the Frenchmen advanced, a sudden thunder of artillery and gunfire came from the fort. In minutes, two French colonels and dozens of infantrymen were cut down. The soldiers kept pressing forward over the bodies of dead comrades. At one point a man climbed the fort's wall and raised the French flag. Mexican defenders quickly killed the invader and tore down the banner. Outside the fort dead French soldiers, dressed in blue and red uniforms, littered the ground. Finally Zaragoza ordered a cavalry charge, which was led by the bold young officer Porfirio Díaz. The French retreated and an immortal chapter was written in Mexican history.

Porfirio Díaz *(Library of Congress)*

In Mexico City President Juárez declared the Fifth of May (*Cinco de Mayo*) to be a national holiday, and it has been a festival day ever since. On May 5, 1862, a supposedly weak Mexican army defeated a force of foreign invaders. To military experts around the world the Mexican victory was shocking. How did a rag-tag band of soldiers defeat Europe's finest troops? Certainly Zaragoza was a clever general while Lorencez acted in a brash manner. But another factor could have been at play in the Battle of Puebla. In the past Mexican soldiers fought for a president who was both white and from upper-class circumstances. This time the Indian and mestizo infantrymen fought for a president of their own background, a man of the people.

Napoleon III and his staff in France were stunned by the loss at Puebla. Some one thousand men under General Lorencez were killed outside of Fort Guadalupe. It marked the first French military defeat in fifty years. Still, the Emperor's pride would not allow him to abandon his Mexican adventure. He sent 30,000 of his best soldiers to Mexico. In early March 1863 the French Army fought a second Battle of Puebla. This

Cinco de Mayo

Today Cinco de Mayo (Fifth of May) is celebrated in Mexico and by Mexicans living in foreign lands. Many Americans mistake the Battle of Puebla festivities with Mexican Independence Day, which falls on September 16.

Some observers claim Cinco de Mayo is celebrated with greater enthusiasm by Mexicans living in the United States than by those in their own country. A theory says this is true because Ignacio Zaragoza was born in Texas while Texas was still a province of Mexico. Therefore Zaragoza was, in effect, a Mexican American. Ignacio Zaragoza was a bright young man who probably would have advanced in Mexican society, but he caught typhus shortly after the Battle of Puebla and died of the disease at age thirty-three.

time French soldiers surrounded the town and its forts. After two months the Mexican defenders, out of food and ammunition, were forced to surrender. One of the captured officers was Porfirio Díaz. He managed to escape a prisoner of war camp, and would later return to battle the French.

President Juárez had little choice but to flee from the capital after the French triumph during the second Battle of Puebla. On May 31, 1863, Juárez stood in the Zocalo, the broad plaza in central Mexico City, and watched soldiers haul down the flag of Mexico. The soldiers handed the rolled up flag to their president. He kissed the banner and cried out *Viva Mexico!* Those watching the flag ceremony understood its deeper meaning. This quiet little Indian, who was not known for dramatic gestures, kissed his country's flag and turned loss into triumph. Clearly he was determined to return

A Mexican flag flying in the zocalo of Mexico City

to the capital someday, raise the flag again, and proclaim a free Mexico. The story of his devotion to his country spread from the capital and was told in towns and villages. Juárez fled, riding his black carriage northward from Mexico City. As he traveled people lined the roads and greeted him with chants: "Viva Juárez! Viva Juárez! Viva Juárez!"

EIGHT

The Crown of Mexico

Well before the victory of his army, Napoleon III sought a man to serve as emperor over Mexico. He chose the Austrian archduke Ferdinand Maximilian von Hapsburg. Born in 1832 into the powerful Hapsburg family, Maximilian suffered one great misfortune: his brother, Franz Joseph, was two years older than he. Therefore the older brother was destined to rule. Franz Joseph became Emperor of Austria in 1848, at age eighteen, and headed that nation for the next sixty-eight years. Meanwhile the younger Hapsburg brother, Maximilian, was a prince without a throne.

Hapsburg family members were primarily of German blood. The mighty Hapsburgs had served as rulers in Europe since 1273 when a family member, Count Rudolf, became Holy Roman Emperor. One of the most famous of the Hapsburgs was the Austrian Empress María Theresa (1717–1780). María Theresa built the magnificent Schönbrunn Palace in Vienna.

Ferdinand Maximilian von Hapsburg *(Library of Congress)*

Ferdinand Maximilian von Hapsburg was born in there in 1832.

Tall and blond, Maximilian attended the finest schools and served as an officer in the Austrian navy. In 1857 he married the Belgian princess Charlotte, called Carlota in Spanish. The attractive young couple were popular guests in the ballrooms of Europe. Proper bearing and fine appearance made Maximilian and Carlota the perfect image of an emperor and an empress.

Napoleon's wife Eugénie engineered the French occupation of Mexico.
(Library of Congress)

The intrigue which put the royal couple in Mexico began in the court of Napoleon III. Napoleon's wife, Eugénie, was a behind-the-scenes manipulator in French power politics. In those days it was unusual for the wife of an emperor to play a strong role in a nation's foreign policy. But Napoleon made a compromise. The French Emperor kept a string of girlfriends on close call. Many historians believe Napoleon granted his wife a position of influence in exchange for her forgiving his affairs with other women. Therefore Eugénie was given Mexico as a plaything as long as she overlooked her husband's antics in the bedroom.

In 1862, Eugénie and Napoleon entertained a charming guest, José Manuel Hidalgo of Mexico. Hidalgo was born into a wealthy Mexican family which had sided with the conservatives. He and his family lost their fortune during the War of the Reform. He now lived as an exile in Paris with several other well-to-do Mexican men and women. A persuasive talker, Hidalgo convinced Eugénie that the Mexican people would obey and eventually learn to love a prince sent to Mexico by the French. Such a prince would have to be Catholic and move to restore the powers of the church.

Maximilian and Carlota, both Catholics, were called to Napoleon's chambers where they were presented the crown of Mexico as if it were a gift. At first Maximilian was reluctant to accept the position of emperor in a far-flung land. Carlota, who adored her husband, persuaded him to sign on to the mission. She wanted to see Maximilian take his place among the great royal rulers of the world. Besides, he was a Hapsburg and was born to occupy a throne. Finally Maximilian agreed, but only if the Mexican people approved. Hidalgo, the persuasive Mexican, assured him a vote would be taken and the Mexicans would welcome him as their ruler.

A great party was held in Miramar, Maximilian's palace near the Austrian city of Triest. Maximilian loved Miramar Castle and at heart did not wish to leave his comfortable home. But overriding all other considerations was the fact that he was a Hapsburg. As a Hapsburg, he felt a higher duty called him to Mexico. Also his wife, Carlota, brimmed with

Maximilian was persuaded to accept the emperorship of Mexico by his wife Carlota. *(Library of Congress)*

excitement over the Mexican undertaking. Surrounded by dignitaries, both Mexican and European, Maximilian signed the documents making him the Emperor of Mexico. For the ceremony he wore the uniform of the Austrian Navy and Carlota wore a pretty pink dress. After the signing a band played the Mexican National Anthem. It was April 10, 1864, a date that sealed Maximilian's fate.

The people of Triest were saddened to lose Maximilian and Carlota. The royal couple enjoyed the love of common-ers. On Sundays they opened their palace gardens for the people to walk about. They attended weddings and baptismal parties held by the peasants, never showing the arrogance so often displayed by other members of European royalty. Some Miramar neighbors grimly predicted a dire future for Maximilian in a wild country such as Mexico. The words of a drinking song sung in Triest taverns went:

> *Do not trust them, Maximilian!*
> *Turn back, go back to Miramar!*

In the spring Maximilian and Carlota boarded the warship *Novara* to begin the thirty-seven day journey from Europe to Mexico. As promised a vote was taken, and Maximilian was told that more than 6 million Mexicans signed a petition endorsing him to be Emperor of Mexico. He did not know the petition was a fraud. Mexico did not hold 6 million people who were literate enough to sign their names on such a document. Still, excitement reigned aboard the ship *Novara*. Maximilian and Carlota, the proud offspring of the European aristocracy, were off to rule Mexico and bring peace and happiness to the people. He was thirty-two years old and she twenty-four.

The royal couple's disappointment began at the port city of Veracruz when they arrived in May 1864. They expected to be greeted by a host of officials and perhaps by a military band. Instead no one received them at the waterfront. Veracruz had always been a liberal town. In fact, many Mexicans viewed the entire French intervention as a continuation of the liberal and conservative fight featured in the War of the Reform. Liberals sided with Juárez and looked upon Maximilian as a conservative Mexican politician disguised as a European monarch.

Carlota was so heartbroken at the coldness of the Veracruz reception that she broke down and cried. Adding to the royal couple's gloom was a defiant letter from Juárez which they received two days after their arrival. At the time Juárez was far to the north, near the border with the United States. He warned, "[Those who] attack the rights of others, seize their goods, assault the lives of those who defend their nationality [shall face] the tremendous judgment of history."

Despite their growing fears, Maximilian and Carlota boarded a coach for the long, bumpy ride to Mexico City. Over Mexico's primitive road system the trip from Veracruz to the capital took two weeks. At the town of Orizaba they found paper flyers passed out to the people which read, "Long live the Republic, long live Independence, death to the Emperor."

The travelers brightened at Puebla, scene of the heroic Fifth of May Battle. There the couple encountered Indians who greeted them, not with applause but with friendly smiles. Indians remembered the story of the god Quetzalcoatl, who was depicted in ancient paintings as a blond white man with a beard. Maximilian was a blue-eyed blond who sported a carefully combed beard. Legends said the god Quetzalcoatl once ruled Mexico and was kind to the people. A rival god drove Quetzalcoatl off the land, but he vowed to return some day to claim Mexico as his rightful possession. Many Indians now wondered if Maximilian was the returning god, fulfilling his ancient promise.

Outside of Mexico City, Carlota stopped at the shrine of Guadalupe. This was sacred ground, for here stood the church dedicated to the woman hailed as the mother of all Mexicans. Hundreds watched as the couple approached the painting of Guadalupe, which many believed was rendered by angels. A hush prevailed when Maximilian and Carlota

A depiction of Maximilian and Carlotta kneeling before the Virgin of Guadalupe *(Library of Congress)*

dropped to their knees, bowed their heads, and prayed to the Virgin. They did this in a humble manner as if they were common farmers or even beggars. This act of homage to the Virgin won the hearts of devout Mexicans who regarded the couple as Catholic saviors.

Mexico City greeted Maximilian and Carlota with a triumphant reception. They rode in a coach at the head of a parade while men set off fireworks and women stood on balconies showering them with flowers. At the Zocalo in the center of the city, there stood French soldiers in precision ranks. On this spot, just months earlier, Juárez kissed the flag and retreated to the north. People cheered their president then, and now the notoriously changeable Mexico City crowds applauded their new emperor and empress. In the masses at the Zocalo was the young college student Justo Sierra. He reported the people were charmed by Maximilian, "With his slender figure, his benign and clear-eyed expression, he was quite attractive, and the populace felt his magnetism. Carlota, very tall and straight, with her intelligent and penetrating gaze seemed more masculine than her husband."

Only one mishap dimmed the couple's first night in Mexico City. No one told the servants to clean the couple's apartment in the presidential quarters. The apartment had been vacant for many months. Mice in the quarters were so annoying that Maximilian was forced to sleep on a billiards table.

Just a week after his arrival in the capital, Maximilian rode on horseback to visit Chapultepec Castle on the outskirts of the city. The castle had been built in the 1780s to house the viceroys of Spain. It recently served as a military academy, but now stood vacant and in disrepair. Maximilian began refurbishing the structure at once, hoping one day it would rise as proud and as grand as the best royal palaces in Europe. The castle stood on a flat-topped hill in Chapultepec Park, which was once a private hunting ground for Aztec kings. The park contained groves of lovely 1,000-year-old cypress trees. Its forest setting, which offered striking views of the city, fired Maximilian's imagination. About the castle he wrote his younger brother, "It [will be] the Schönbrunn of Mexico,

Chapultepec Castle *(Library of Congress)*

an enchanting pleasure palace built on basalt rock surrounded by the gigantic and famous trees of Montezuma."

As Maximilian moved into his palace, Benito Juárez was homeless and in flight. The French military had troops roaming

Contrasting Carriages

Chapultepec Castle today houses The Museum of Mexican History and is open to the public. Among the displays are two carriages: one used by Emperor Maximilian and the other by President Juárez. Maximilian's coach is gilded and decorated with exquisite carvings. The carriage used by Juárez is plain and black. The two coaches symbolize the opposite backgrounds of the two men—one born a European prince, the other a simple shepherd boy.

the country with orders to arrest him. Juárez, traveling in his signature black coach, retreated northward. With Mexico under foreign occupation, even many of his own people rejected their president. At the outskirts of Monterrey in the north an advanced party requested a four-gun salute when President Juárez entered the city. The mayor of Monterrey was reluctant to comply with the request as he was doing a thriving contraband business with the pro-French American Confederates. Cannons were set up, but as the Juárez coach approached, opponents stole the guns and fired at the Juárez party. His own officers urged the President to speed his carriage out of town, but Juárez objected to such a frenzied flight. He told his driver to spur the horses forward, "At a trot. The President of the Republic cannot run."

Finally Juárez set up a government-in-exile at Paso del Norte, a town on the border with the United States. His presidency as well as his personal life sank to a tragic low point. Margarita and the children took refuge in the United States. At first the family lived in Washington, D.C., and then they moved to New York City, and eventually to the town of New

A nineteenth-century photograph of Paso del Norte *(Library of Congress)*

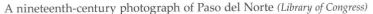

Rochelle, New York. Abraham Lincoln and the North favored Juárez, and she was well treated by government officials. She was even the guest of honor at a White House diner given by Secretary of State William Seward. But Margarita had no friends or relatives in her new circumstances. She spoke no English and disliked the cold New York climate. Worst yet, two of her children sickened and died while in the United States. In a letter to her husband Margarita blamed her own incompetence for the deaths. Juárez read the letter many times, searching for hidden meanings in the words. He feared his wife was going insane.

In 1864, a year of gloom, Juárez must have questioned his mission in life. He was president of his nation, but he was forced to live like a fugitive hiding in a tiny border town. Since he entered politics his family was frequently on the run, escaping from one enemy or another. The strain on his family and the recent deaths of two sons saddened him beyond measure. In his stoic manner he tried to put up a brave front as he felt a president must. Yet his soul was in torment. At a dinner party given to him by his supporters, one guest proposed a toast to the family of President Benito Juárez. Juárez raised his glass to join the toast, but he then broke down and sobbed.

Juárez City

In 1888 the town of Paso del Norte (The Northern Pass) was renamed Ciudad Juárez (Juárez City). For decades it remained a small town, but began to grow in the 1950s. Sitting directly across the Rio Grande River from El Paso, Texas, Ciudad Juárez now holds some 1.1 million inhabitants and is the fifth-largest city in Mexico.

In Mexico City, Emperor Maximilian began the task of governing his country. His approach shocked many Mexicans, especially the conservatives. Like Juárez, he proposed to build schools and educate every Mexican boy and girl. He signed laws forbidding child labor. He moved to lessen the power the military had over the people. He even spoke of reaching out to Benito Juárez, and asking him to serve in a high position of government. It was rumored that Maximilian wanted Juárez to be the Empire's prime minister. Most stunning of all, Maximilian refused to restore property and power to the Catholic Church of Mexico.

Maximilian was a man of his century and liberalism was the driving force of the times. He was a liberal in that he believed a nation's government must be run for the benefit of the people, including the poorest of the society. The Emperor made one major exception to liberal thought: He believed kings and queens—people born into their position—made the best rulers. Poor, confused Mexico was an example of a country in dire need of royal care. The chronic civil wars which plagued the land were led by men hungry for power. An emperor, whose power could not be questioned, would put an end to strife prompted by political rivalry. Maximilian once wrote, "The institution of monarchy is the only one suitable to Mexico . . . because it combines order with liberty, and strength with the strictest justification."

Funds came from Napoleon in France to meet the costs of governing the Mexican Empire. Maximilian launched several public projects. In Mexico City he began construction of a broad, straight road from his palace in Chapultepec to the Zocalo downtown. That roadway became the Paseo de la Reforma. At the time Napoleon III was engaged in rebuilding Paris into the city of marvelous boulevards that we know today. The Reforma was Mexico City's touch of Paris. Maximilian also backed the construction of a railroad linking the capital to the port of Veracruz. Such a railroad had been the dream of Benito Juárez. The United States already enjoyed a railway system which stretched many thousands of miles. Maximilian believed it was time his Mexico began catching up with its northern neighbor.

In addition to public projects, Maximilian spent freely on enhancing his own court. He lavished money rebuilding Chapultepec Castle. From Europe came fine paintings and statutes to dignify the castle's rooms and hallways. Carlota chose much of the Castle's artwork. Entertainment expenses soared. In Maximilian's first six months in office he hosted twenty banquets, seventy lunches, and sixteen grand balls.

During his first six months as emperor, Maximilian spent huge amounts of money on extravagant parties and lavish balls. (*Library of Congress*)

His wine bill alone was more than 100,000 pesos, a price that would feed hundreds of Mexican families for many months. Curiously, Maximilian claimed he did not enjoy the banquets and the balls. He said he gave these parties only for the benefit of guests, which included European dignitaries, French army officers, and upper class Mexicans. Carlota, on the other hand, was a superb dancer and loved the festivals given in Chapultepec Castle.

Billiards and the Emperor

Maximilian's favorite form of recreation was to play pool with other men. The billiards table in Chapultepec Castle stood on four thick legs. It was a custom at Chapultepec that when an opponent lost a pool game he was compelled, as a joke, to crawl under the table on hands and knees. When Emperor Maximilian lost, his man servant did the crawling.

The Emperor and Empress tried to become Mexican in every way. They wore Mexican style clothes and at meals ate tortillas instead of bread. In letters home they used phrases such as "we" Mexicans and "you" Europeans. On September 16, 1864, Maximilian journeyed to the town of Dolores. There he stood on the same church step where fifty-four years earlier Father Hidalgo proclaimed independence. On that historic spot the Austrian-born emperor delivered a passionate speech hailing the heroes who fought Spain for Mexico's freedom.

Many Mexicans found the gestures of the royal couple to be admirable. Maximilian and Carlota were truly well

Mariachis, The Positive Legacy of French Occupation

Today Mexico is famous for its mariachi bands. The typical mariachi group has a singer-leader and six to eight members who play horns, violins, and guitars. These groups got their start during the French intervention when French soldiers married Mexican girls and wanted to hire a band to entertain their wedding guests. Mariachi is a corruption of a French word for marriage.

meaning and wanted the best for the Mexican people. But Mexicans also realized that before the Europeans arrived their country had a constitution and a president. The constitution represented a great stride taken by the nation. Now this magnificent step forward was dashed by a foreign emperor. It meant little that the emperor attempted to rule in an honorable manner. He remained an invader who upset the constitution and ousted the legitimate president. So, Mexicans smiled and politely applauded their emperor and empress. They had little choice but to show respect as French troops were quick to punish any act of rebellion. Still, a secret dream burned in their hearts. Some day that courageous man, who they called the little Indian, would return, and raise the flag of Mexico over their nation's capital.

NINE

The Fall of the Crown

I n France, Napoleon III seethed. The French Empire he hoped to build in Mexico was proving to be a disaster. Ferdinand Maximilian, his hand-chosen emperor, was spending a fortune in French money with little benefit to France. Mexican conservatives complained to Napoleon that Maximilian acted more like a liberal than did Juárez.

Especially frustrating was Maximilian's attitude towards the church. He refused to return property the liberals confiscated from the Mexican Catholic Church, and he would not restore the legal privileges (the *fueros*) the priests once enjoyed. In the spring of 1865 an angry Napoleon III wrote Maximilian, "Mexico owes her independence and her present regime to France, but it looks as if some mysterious influence is always stepping in to prevent French agents from devoting themselves to the good of the country."

Also disturbing for Napoleon was the fact that Benito Juárez, the constitutional president, simply would not go

After a Confederate surrender ended the Civil War, American troops were able to concentrate on expelling French forces from Mexico. *(Library of Congress)*

away. From his headquarters in Paso del Norte, Juárez commanded a small but loyal army. The president's office printed communiqués which were circulated throughout the country and read in secrecy. Anyone caught reading Juárez' bulletins could be jailed by French authorities. On January 1, 1865, Juárez issued a statement confidently telling his countrymen the French-backed regime would soon fall: "Mexicans: After three years of unequal and bloody struggle against the foreign armies occupying our country, we are now on our feet, ready to defend our independence and liberty against the despots."

A dire event for both Napoleon and Maximilian took place hundreds of miles to the north of Mexico. In the United States, the Union General Ulysses Grant seized Richmond, Virginia which served as the capital of the Confederacy. On April 9,

1865, the Confederates surrendered to Grant at Appomattox Court House. The American Civil War was over.

From the beginning the United States made public its displeasure over the French intervention in Mexico. The establishment of a European-led monarchy in America's close neighbor was a clear violation of the Monroe Doctrine. Now that the Civil War had ended, the United States was free to push Maximilian and the French out of Mexico. At the time the United States commanded the strongest army and navy in the world. The French had 30,000 soldiers stationed in Mexico, and they would be no match for the battle-hardened American infantry.

Lincoln and Juárez

Abraham Lincoln was assassinated just days after the official end of the Civil War. They never met, but historians have long noted many similarities between the two leaders. Lincoln was born in 1809, just three years after Juárez' birth. Both men grew up in poverty and struggled to get an education. Both were lawyers. Both led their countries through bitter and bloody civil wars.

Abraham Lincoln

In the summer of 1865, the United States began to mass troops on the northern side of the Rio Grande. Thousands of rifles and many cases of ammunition were left in convenient dumps where Juárez' forces could take them. These were modern firearms, and they bolstered the President's army. Slowly soldiers loyal to Juárez marched out of northern Mexico to begin a reconquest of the land.

Maximilian and Carlota coped with the coming crisis by devoting their lives even more to Mexico, their adopted country. Carlota made a public show of decorating Mexico City's Alemeda Park with bright flowers. Her court of ladies-in-waiting became increasingly staffed by pretty young Mexican girls. Maximilian studied Indian languages, hoping to win the native people over to his side. For years previous governments had stripped the Indians of their traditional lands. Maximilian passed laws returning those lands. In 1865, he established a commission to listen to Indian complaints. Maximilian wrote, "The best are and continue to be the Indians."

In return, the Emperor won the gratitude and even the loyalty of many Indian people. Maximilian was the first white man in high government circles to reach out to the Indian community. As the war with Juárez' forces grew in intensity, Maximilian's bravest general was Tomás Mejía, the Indian chieftain. Mejía fought for the restoration of Catholic power. Although Maximilian was not inclined to elevate the church, Mejía believed Europeans would eventually give Catholic priests a stronger say in government.

Maximilian and Carlota were childless, which meant they were royal rulers without an heir. In September 1865, the couple announced they were adopting three-year-old Agustín de Iturbide. The young boy was the grandson of the first emperor of Mexico, the man who led the country after independence. Maximilian and Carlota believed the adoption would give the Empire a solid foundation. They now had an heir, someone to take over leadership in the event of their deaths. And this heir was from an illustrious Mexican family.

Maximilian reached out to Juárez. Publicly he asked Juárez, "to come to me and faithfully assist me." This was a sincere offer on the emperor's part. Maximilian was willing to let Juárez join his government. He did not mention exactly what office he wanted to give Juárez, but it made no difference. Juárez never replied to the Maximilian offers. As a man of law, he stood by the 1857 constitution. That document made him—not the Austrian archduke—the proper leader of Mexico.

The war against the French was fought on battlefields and in the villages as a guerilla war. Juárez's agents smuggled arms into towns and farming communities. French soldiers lived in a state of constant terror. Snipers shot them down and bands of village warriors attacked small French units. The guerilla warfare infuriated Maximilian. He called the rural people who attacked his soldiers bandits and madmen who wished to bring chaos to Mexico. On October 3, 1865, Maximilian signed what became known as the Black Decree, a document condemning hundreds of Mexicans.

The Black Decree stated that anyone caught in possession of an illegal firearm could be put to death. Violators received no trial. Execution by firing squad was a decision made by local French commanders. A proclamation spelling out the measures of the Black Decree said, "The time for indulgence has passed, for it would only help the despotism of the bandits . . . The government, strong and powerful, will henceforth impose inflexible punishment."

Maximilian's actions since he had come to Mexico indicated that he was motivated by a desire to govern in a fair and humane way—as defined by European standards. His attempts to reach out to the native peoples and his willingness to exert some control over the powerful Catholic Church were in the best European enlightened tradition. But his signing of the Black Decree, and the brutal way it was enforced, reveals another side to his rule, a side that was also characteristic of how Europeans often ruled in countries far away from Europe.

Maximilian was apparently unable to realize that, regardless of how benevolent his rule was, the Mexican people wanted the right to self-determination. When a sizable portion of the population continued to resist his rule, despite what he saw as his generosity and humanitarian intentions, he grew increasingly frustrated. Now that his control over Mexico had been put in real peril, he reverted into more of a traditional Hapsburg. In this tradition, emperors conducted themselves as proper fathers, which meant they should act in a firm manner when the king decided firmness was necessary. Emperors ruled by divine authority and, in the end, only he knew what was best; when their subjects needed punishment it was the ruler's sad duty to punish. With the Black Decree, Maximilian set out to carry out that duty, regardless of how many innocent people had to suffer.

In village after village rebels and those suspected of rebel activity were dragged from their homes, lined up against a wall and executed by firing squad. The Black Decree swept Mexico like a killer storm. Still, the war against Maximilian and the French grew in fury. Guerrilla warfare in the countryside could not be stopped even by the mass executions. Justo Sierra wrote, "Moral resistance to the regime born of the French invasion, as well as armed resistance, was growing despite the reign of terror."

The ultimate disaster for Maximilian came early in 1866 with a stunning announcement by Napoleon III. The French Emperor said he had had enough and he was pulling his troops out of Mexico. Napoleon had long been under pressure from the United States to withdraw. His Mexican adventure had never been popular with the French people. Also the neighboring Kingdom of Prussia grew militarily strong. French soldiers stationed in Mexico were needed at home in case a new European war broke out. Finally Napoleon realized his dreams of establishing an empire in Mexico had been dashed—dashed by the liberal-minded and often confused Ferdinand Maximilian.

The royal couple in Mexico City was left shocked and dismayed. Without the protection of the French army the Mexican Empire would certainly fall to Juárez and his guerilla fighters. At first Maximilian believed he should simply leave with the French forces and return to Europe. But Carlota, who was the stronger of the two, would hear no such an argument. Retreating from Mexico would mean abdication, the giving up of a position of leadership. Her husband was a Hapsburg. No Hapsburg had ever abdicated. Napoleon, she believed, would change his mind when he knew the facts regarding the Mexico situation. This, she decided, was her job. She would go to Paris and speak to Napoleon. She could be very persuasive, and was confident she would change Napoleon's thinking.

In July 1866, Carlota boarded a ship at Veracruz to make the voyage to France. Mexicans sang a bittersweet but cynical song about her mission:

> The ship sails, over the seas,
> Bouncing like a ball,
> Farewell, Mamá Carlota,
> Farewell, my sweet love.

In Paris, Napoleon III refused to see Carlota, claiming he was ill. The Empress Eugénie did talk to her, and this was fitting as Eugénie was one of the primary architects of the French intervention in Mexico. But Carlota insisted on an audience with the Emperor. She hinted she would pound and kick on his bedroom door if necessary. Finally Napoleon agreed to a meeting. It was true Napoleon was ill, and talking to Carlota no

doubt worsened his condition. Carlota accused the French Emperor of betraying her husband. During the conversation, Napoleon could do nothing more than apologize for his actions. Several times he broke down and wept with sadness.

In an attempt to regain French aid in Mexico, Carlota traveled to France and sought an audience with Napoleon III. (*Library of Congress*)

Strain and disappointment jarred Carlota's mind. She refused the Emperor's offer of tea because she feared Napoleon wanted to poison her. Napoleon, she concluded, was a demon. From Paris she wrote to her husband, "To me he [Napoleon] is the devil in person."

Not satisfied with taking her case to Napoleon, Carlota traveled to Rome to plead with Pope Pius IX. Perhaps the head of the Catholic Church would aid her cause. On the trip to Rome she refused food and drink because she believed everything offered her was poisoned. At the Vatican, the Pope's headquarters, all she could talk about was her fear that Napoleon was trying to kill her. In front of the Pope she screamed hysterically that Napoleon's assassins lurked

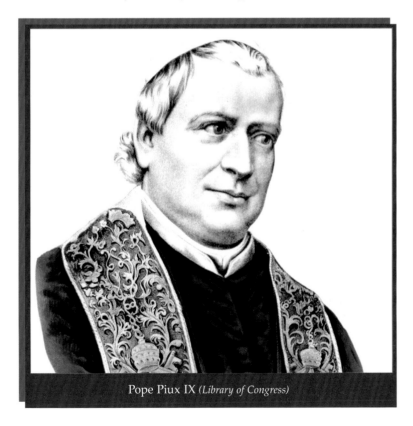

Pope Piux IX (Library of Congress)

everywhere—even in the hallways of the Vatican. Because of her condition Pius IX allowed her to stay the night. It marked the first time, at least according to official records, that a woman slept at the Vatican.

A day after her encounter with the Pope, Carlota wrote her last letter to her husband. Her words reflect a person, marching toward death, and serenely accepting death as the final relief from her world of suffering: "Dearly beloved treasure, I bid you farewell. God is calling me to Him. I thank you for the happiness which you have always given me. May God bless you and help you win eternal bliss."

By March 1867, the last French military unit was gone and Mexico was aflame with war. Guerilla warfare flared

This scene depicts Emperor Maximilian watching as French troops evacuate Mexico. *(Library of Congress)*

everywhere. Juárez' forces advanced southward, fighting those armies that remained loyal to Maximilian despite the French withdraw. Riding in his black coach, Juárez traveled with his soldiers so close to the battlefronts that at one point he was almost captured by the enemy.

Once more Maximilian pondered abdication. Letters arriving from Europe claimed his wife had gone insane. His proud Empire was collapsing on all sides. Still the thought of giving up his throne burned at his very soul. He was a Hapsburg and could never bring disgrace to his family. With his loyal generals Miramón and Mejía, Maximilian rode north to the

When French troops left Mexico, Maximilian took it upon himself to lead those loyal to him in battle against Juárez's insurgent force. *(Library of Congress)*

city of Querétaro. There he was determined to make a last stand. Like the kings of old he would either die on his throne or at least at the head of his army.

For seventy-one days, Maximilian's soldiers held out against Juárez. During many battles Maximilian was seen at the front urging his men to have courage. The end came on the night of May 14, 1867, when a small force of soldiers slipped past sentries and captured Maximilian. When taken prisoner, Maximilian made a great show of presenting his sword to the enemy commanding officer. All military courtesies were respected by both sides. The one-time Emperor was imprisoned in a shed on a rise called the Hill of Bells.

From all over the world, including the United States, came pleas to spare Maximilian's life. A trial was held in a Querétaro theater. By a narrow vote a jury of army officers passed sentence: death by firing squad. As president, Juárez had the power to pardon Maximilian. But Juárez insisted the trial was legal and fair. "I am not the one who has condemned [him]; it is the law, it is the people," Juárez said in a letter. Prosecutors repeatedly bought up the horrors suffered by Mexican people by the Black Decree which was signed by the Emperor. Plus, as Juárez pointed out, foreign aggressors must be taught a lesson they would never forget.

Early in the morning on June 19, 1867, Maximilian and his two generals, Miramón and Mejía, were lined up against a stone wall on the Hill of Bells. Three thousand Mexican soldiers stood in ranks to witness the execution. Maximilian gave each member of the firing squad a gold coin and asked them to aim at his heart. He had made arrangements for his body to be embalmed and shipped home, and he did not want his mother to see any facial wounds. The three men

This Edouard Manet painting shows the execution of Emperor Maximilian, General Miramón, and General Mejía.

stood stiffly at attention waiting their fate. The expression on Maximilian's face was so calm and serene that one observer wrote, "He already seemed to belong to another world." Just before the command was given to fire, Maximilian shouted out, "Viva Mexico!"

On his way through Querétaro, Benito Juárez stopped to view Maximilian's body. The shepherd boy and the crown

The Hill of Bells Today

The Hill of Bells (*Cerro de las Campañas*) is so named because stones found there made a ringing sound, like church bells, when thumped together. Those curious musical stones long ago disappeared.

Today the Hill of Bells in Querétaro is a well-kept park that is often visited by classes of Mexican schoolchildren. The Austrian government put up a tiny chapel on the spot where Maximilian died. On a hill above that chapel stands a towering statue of Juárez erected by the government of Mexico.

prince had never met in life, and Juárez' silent thoughts when standing over his enemy's remains are unknown. Months later Maximilian's corpse was shipped back to Austria to be buried in the Hapsburg family cemetery in Vienna. The coffin crossed the Atlantic on the *Novara*, the same ship that brought Maximilian and Carlota to Mexico three years earlier.

Carlota returned to her family home in Belgium. There she lived in a small castle attended by servants and nurses. She never left the castle grounds. She died in 1927, at the age of eighty-six. As a courtesy she was often visited by members of the Belgium royal family. Rarely did she talk of her husband or her time in Mexico. When visitors inquired as to her health, Carlota spoke about herself in the third person: "one is old, one is stupid, one is mad. The mad woman is still alive."

TEN

The Father of the Country

Mexico City crowds loved a show, and Juárez gave them one on July 15, 1867. Leading a triumphant parade, he rode towards the Zocalo while men and women lined the streets cheering their president. At the Zocalo, Juárez marched to the flagpole and raised the flag of Mexico. A military band played the National Anthem. Fireworks boomed. Those who knew him claimed Juárez seldom smiled. But at the moment the flag reached the top of the pole his smile flashed so bright it could be seen by everyone packed into the broad plaza.

President Juárez had ample reason to smile. His country had endured more than fifty years of war and two invasions by foreign powers. Finally the French, the last of the foreign intruders, had been driven away. Perhaps now Mexico could find peace. In his official pronouncement published on July

15, Juárez compared the moment to when Mexico achieved independence from Spain:

> Mexicans: We have accomplished the greatest good that we could hope for; we have completed our second struggle for independence. Let us all work together to leave to our children the opportunity for prosperity, loving and sustaining always our independence and our liberty.

Dimming the celebration in Mexico City was gloom cast by the specter of recent wars. Justo Sierra described the mood of the times: "The country was a wreck. Everywhere [the wars] had left ruins and squalor amidst pools of blood." Thousands of Mexicans had died in the War of the Reform and in the fighting against the French. The shadow of death lingering everywhere stripped Mexican society of its zeal. Just eight days after the flag-raising ceremony, Juárez wrote to a woman who had lost her husband in the French War: "For me it is a sad and grievous pleasure to receive congratulations with which I am honored by persons to whom the price of triumph of the Republic has been the life of the most beloved of their kindred. Each Mexican who died for his country is to me a brother."

The President's spirits rose with the return of his family. Margarita and her five unmarried daughters and last remaining son arrived in Mexico City in the late summer of 1867. Juárez had feared the recent deaths of two sons depressed Margarita to the point of insanity, but she seemed her old, cheerful self. The children were overjoyed to be back home with their father.

Most dangerous to the future was a culture of war which hung over the country like a storm cloud. At the moment

Mexico had achieved peace and freedom. Not one inch of Mexican soil was ruled by foreigners. But never before in Mexican history were there so many armed men living on the nation's farms and in its villages. Thousands of young men knew no life other than the military. Commanders of various ranks were accustomed to plundering communities to obtain food and horses for their soldiers. The commanders believed military revolt was an acceptable way—perhaps the only way—for them to advance in Mexican society.

One such ambitious general was Porfirio Díaz. Observers noticed a coldness between the general and the president. On the day of the victory parade, Díaz rode to the outskirts of the capital to meet Juárez. Most people expected Juárez to open the carriage door and invite Díaz to join him for the march to the Zocalo. Instead Juárez nodded and said nothing. Díaz was forced to ride in a coach trailing the president's carriage.

General Porfirio Díaz *(Library of Congress)*

Juárez had always distrusted the military. He had known too many generals who were cunning and given to acts of treachery. Too often in the past, military revolts shook Mexico's government and led to civil war. Also armies were expensive to maintain. He would rather spend tax money on a school system. In 1867, the Mexican army had 90,000 men; Juárez promptly dismissed two-thirds of them.

Most of the discharged military men retained their weapons, and many found they could not adjust to civilian life. Hundreds of ex-soldiers became bandits and turned Mexican roads into a hell of killing, robbery, and kidnapping. Juárez organized a special police force, called the *Rurales*, to patrol the country roads. The Rurales thought little of shooting down bandits without benefit of a trial.

To combat the rampant banditry on Mexican roads, Juárez instituted a special road patrol force known as Los Rurales. *(Library of Congress)*

One-time soldiers attached themselves to aggressive commanders. In turn, the commanders carved out chunks of Mexican territory and ruled like petty dictators. Juárez, always a stickler when it came to legal principals, believed the rebellious military chieftains were lawbreakers who must be punished. He dealt with the military upstarts as harshly as he did with Maximilian. Showing no pity, he ordered the Mexican army to crush enclaves governed by ex-generals and to execute all who resisted. The severe measures he imposed on rebel generals led many liberal historians to charge that Juárez ruled as a dictator in his later years. President Juárez always maintained he only acted in such a way as to uphold the law.

Special elections were held in 1867 and Juárez was reelected to the office of President. Technically he was not the president at the time of the flag-raising ceremony because his term of office expired December 1, 1865. However, on that date, Emperor Maximilian ruled Mexico and President Juárez had taken refuge in Paso del Norte. Given those circumstances it was impossible for the legitimate government to hold elections. Most Mexicans agreed that Juárez was president by default during the French intervention years, but the fact that his term had expired gave fuel to his many rivals.

One of Juárez's most ambitious projects was completing the railroad line between the port of Veracruz and the capital. Such a line was planned as early as the 1830s and worked upon off and on since the 1850s. The railroad took the same path as did Aztec traders and the conquistador Hernan Cortés. Tracks had to climb over mountains and leap across rivers on bridges. Building the railroad was one of the most difficult engineering feats in progress anywhere in the world at the time. After great expenditures of money and effort the railway between Veracruz and Mexico City opened in 1873.

In national office, Juárez cut wasteful government spending and tried to balance the budget. Bringing responsibility to chaotic financial conditions was always one of his greatest strengths as a government leader. He personally lived within his means and he expected the government and high officials to follow his example. But Mexico's debts were staggering. Years of war had ruined the economy, and tax revenue was almost nonexistent. Justo Sierra said, "The urban masses, their factories and workshops shut down or idle from fear of war or for lack of markets, lapsed into vagrancy."

President Juárez tried to get the economy moving again by encouraging foreign investment. The Veracruz to Mexico City railroad was largely financed and engineered by British banks. Juárez reasoned that since Mexicans lacked the funds to finance construction projects, he had to turn to foreign investors. But the profits on projects such as the new railroad quickly left Mexico and enriched the foreigners. Masses of Mexicans lived in poverty while a few overseas investors made fortunes from Mexico.

Providing an education for Mexican children remained his broadest goal. During the Juárez presidency Mexico built 5,000 schools. By 1874, a record 350,000 Mexican boys and girls attended school, however the country's school-age population totaled almost 2 million. There simply were not enough qualified teachers available, nor did Mexico have proper teacher training colleges. Juárez blamed this dismal state of affairs on the Catholic Church, which had dominated Mexican education for generations. In the past, Catholic teachers concentrated primarily on educating future priests or children of the upper classes. Although Juárez continued to be a devout Catholic, he was especially bitter that Indians were denied schooling under the old system. He once said to Justo Sierra, "I would like to see the Indians converted to Protestantism; they need a religion that will teach them to read and not waste their pennies on candles for the saints."

Margarita Juárez suffered from illnesses her doctors were unable to treat. Letters indicate that Benito Juárez blamed his wife's condition on stress caused largely by his high position in government. Over his years as leader of an unstable country, Mrs. Juárez was forced to move frequently. She was often short of money, and she recently suffered the death of two sons while living in the cold climate of the northern United States. On January 2, 1871, Margarita Juárez sickened and died. She was only forty-four years old. A day after her death Juárez held a funeral to which only family members were invited. Outside the funeral hall in Mexico City thousands of people gathered, heads bowed in silence. A newspaper reporter observing the scene said, "We have never seen a similar unanimity of feelings or an equal expression of sorrow among all classes of the population, without regard to party, opinion, or Nationality."

Juárez, as was his practice, said nothing about his inner feelings regarding the death of his wife. Certainly he was devastated. He had lost his love as well as his most trusted and best friend.

In 1871, Juárez surprised many of his associates when he announced he would run for an unprecedented fourth term as president. His rivals raised the cry that by hanging on to the presidency, Juárez was becoming a dictator. Porfirio Díaz wrote, "Indefinite reelection endangers our national institutions . . . no citizen should perpetuate himself in office." Justo Sierra hailed Juárez' decision to seek a fourth term. According to Sierra, Juárez considered it his duty to retain his office and provide stability at a time when Mexico seemed to be slipping into another civil war. Juárez knew his rivals would accuse him of being power-mad, but he was ready to face that tempest. As Sierra wrote, "Once again he [Juárez] showed himself to be made of bronze, which hurricanes could shake but could not move."

Three men ran for president in 1871: Juárez, Porfirio Díaz, and Sebastián Lerdo de Tejado. The election stood as proof that Mexico was not becoming a dictatorship under Benito Juárez. A true dictator, such as those in Mexico's past, would have defied the constitution and forbade an election. Lerdo's seeking office was somewhat of a surprise as he was a high government official who had always been a close ally of Juárez. But Lerdo was driven by ambition and desired the presidency. No candidate won a majority of votes, so the election was decided by the congress. Juárez won by a small margin. Lerdo was named president of the supreme court. A thoroughly disgusted Porfirio Díaz stormed off to his large house in Oaxaca.

As was true in the past, a close election served as a prelude to disorder. Porfirio Díaz claimed the election was fraudulent and declared himself president. Following customs of the past, Díaz "proclaimed" himself Mexico's leader and expected others to follow his orders. Juárez, always a man of law, fought the Díaz proclamation. He sent an army to Oaxaca which smashed the revolt and killed many of Diáz's private soldiers. Díaz himself escaped capture by dressing in the disguise of a priest and dashing into the countryside. However Díaz's own brother, Félix Díaz, was one of his officers and was killed by the Juárez army during the Oaxaca revolt. The death of a beloved brother increased the hatred Porfirio Díaz felt toward his onetime liberal ally, Benito Juárez.

On March 21, 1872, Benito Juárez turned sixty-six. He had enjoyed good health most of his life, but companions

Some Tributes to Juárez

❑ March 21, Juárez's birthday, is *Dia de Juárez*, (Juárez Day), a national holiday in Mexico.

❑ Mexico's busiest airport is the Benito Juárez Airport outside Mexico City.

❑ Hundreds of schools in Mexico are named for Juárez.

❑ The Benito Juárez Monument, a graceful sculpture, dominates the Alameda Park in central Mexico City; the monument overlooks Avenue Juárez.

❑ The Benito Juárez High School in Chicago, Illinois serves thousands of students, including many in the city's immigrant Mexican community.

❑ In 1969 a statue of Juárez was erected in Washington, D.C.; the statue was part of a government exchange agreement that saw a statue of Abraham Lincoln put up in Mexico City.

❑ In addition to Ciudad Juárez in northern Mexico, more than twenty Mexican towns and villages have Juárez in their names.

❑ In 1883 an Italian socialist living in the town of Dovia, Italy, named his newborn baby boy Benito because he so admired the Mexican leader; the boy grew up to be Benito Mussolini, a Fascist dictator of Italy, and the political opposite of Benito Juárez.

noticed his once brisk walking pace had slowed consider-
ably. His shoulders slumped. Sometimes he complained of
chest pains.

Saying he felt ill, Juárez left his Mexico City office early on
July 18, 1872, and went home. The break in routine caused a
stir among his staff as the President's work habits were rigid.
Almost never did he leave paperwork tasks on his desk to
be taken up the next day. At home he felt staggering chest
pains, and his daughters called in a doctor. "Is my illness
mortal?" Juárez asked. The doctor explained he had a heart
condition and, indeed, it probably was mortal. Juárez then

The tomb of Juárez (Library of Congress)

told the doctor about his boyhood in his Oaxacan village. He recalled how he could always run faster than the other boys and jump higher than them too. The Juarez children were in and out of his bedroom, but when he died later that night only a teenage servant boy sat at his bedside. The boy cried for hours.

Juárez's death ushered in war and turmoil as rivals fought for his office. The peaceful transition of power from one leader to the next was still a painfully difficult accomplishment in Mexico. The head of the supreme court, Lerdo de Tejada, succeeded Juárez as president, but rivals continued to fight each other for the office. In 1877, Porfirio Díaz seized control of Mexico and held the country in his iron fist for the better part of thirty years. Díaz ushered in order through a policy called *pan y palo* (bread or the club). This policy told all military men and officeholders: cooperate with me and you will eat; fail to cooperate and you will be beaten. Under Porfirio Díaz, a form of stability came to Mexico, but democracy gave way to dictatorship. Díaz was overthrown during the civil war of 1910-1920, Mexico's bloodiest revolution.

After Juárez's death, Sebastian Lerdo de Tejada became president.

The Mexican Revolution *(Library of Congress)*

Benito Juárez was born when Mexico was a colony of Spain. He grew up in a time when land ownership and money allowed one Mexican to lord over another as if in a master-and-slave relationship. In his youth, the mestizos lived as second-class citizens and Indians had an even lower status. Juárez brought his own revolution to the nation, a revolution based on law. He supported laws designed to promote racial equality and guarantee Mexican citizens the right to choose their religion. His term as the nation's only full-blooded Indian president was itself a revolution. He gave Mexican society basic freedoms, including freedom of the press. Newspapers, many of which were severely critical of his actions as president, were allowed to print what they wished while he was in office.

Juárez did not achieve peace in his lifetime. But he put Mexico on the path to becoming a modern state, one ruled by laws and not by the whims of men. In the years after his death, Juárez's place in the hearts of Mexicans soared. Because of his vision, Mexicans now hail Benito Juárez as the father of their country.

One of the many statues of Benito Juárez in Mexico

Timeline

1806 Born on March 21 in village of San Pablo Guelatao, state of Oaxaca.

1810 Miguel Hidalgo y Castilla issues a call for Mexican independence on September 15.

1818 Leaves home and takes up residence in the city of Oaxaca.

1821 Mexico wins independence from Spain.

1828 Begins to study law.

1831 Finishes courses and begins to practice law.

1833 Elected a deputy in the Oaxaca state legislature.

1836 General Santa Anna defeats the Alamo defenders in San Antonio, Texas.

1843 Marries Margarita Maza.

1846 –1848 War rages between Mexico and the United States; Mexico loses its northern territories.

1847 Becomes governor of the state of Oaxaca.

1849 Reelected as governor.

1853 Banished from Mexico by Antonio López de Santa Anna; lives in New Orleans.

1854 The Plan of Ayutla, a three-step proposal to restore the Mexican government, published.

1855 Returns to Mexico.

1857 Writes a new constitution with other Mexican leaders; the War of the Reform or Three Years War begins; becomes president of the supreme court, an office next in line to the presidency.

1858 Becomes constitutional president after President Ignacio Commonfort leaves office.

1860 War of the Reform ends.

1861 American Civil War begins; reelected as president.

1862 Small Mexican force defeats a French army at the Battle of Puebla on May 5.

1863 Flees northward after French armies march into Mexico City and install Maximilian von Hapsburg as emperor.

1865 American Civil War ends; Maximilian issues Black Decree which condemns many Mexicans to death by firing squad.

1866 French army ordered out of Mexico by Napoleon III.

1867 Assumes the presidency, once again, after Maximilian captured and executed.

1871 Reelected as president; Porfirio Díaz begins a rebellion.

1872 Dies on July 18.

1877 Porfirio Díaz seizes power in Mexico and rules as a dictator for the next thirty years.

Sources

CHAPTER ONE: The Student Meets the General

p. 12, "with his bare feet . . ." Charles Allen Smart, *Viva Juárez!* (New York: J. B. Lippincott Company, 1963), 61.

CHAPTER TWO: The Zapotec Shepherd Boy

p. 14, "treated him badly and . . . Smart, *Viva Juárez!* 31.

p. 16, "The Spanish language was . . ." Jorge L. Tamayo, ed., *Antología de Benito Juárez* (Mexico City: Universidad Nacional Autónoma de Mexico, 1972), 2

p. 17, "I was left under . . ." Ibid., 2.

p. 17, "as soon as I . . ." Ibid.

p. 18, "his character was obedient . . ." Smart, *Viva Juárez!* 31.

p. 18, "In the few spare . . ." Tamayo, *Antología de Benito Juárez*, 2.

p. 18, "when my uncle called . . ." Ibid.

p. 18-19, "back then it was . . ." Ibid.

p. 20, "I believed that . . ." Ibid., 3.

p. 21, "Also, I too was . . ." Ibid.

p. 22, "There lived in the . . ." Ibid.

p. 23, "In this manner . . ." Ibid., 4.

p. 23, "I spoke the Spanish . . ." Ibid.

p. 24, "Oaxaca was a city . . ." Enrique Krause, *Mexico: Biography of Power* (New York: Harper Collins, 1997), 161.

p. 26, "very humble . . ." Ralph Roeder, *Juárez and His*

Mexico (New York: The Viking Press, 1947), 10.
p. 28, "I was dissatisfied . . ." Smart, *Viva Juárez!* 38.
p. 28, "And this one . . ." Ibid., 51.

CHAPTER THREE: Independence and a New Mexico
p. 35, "You had to hear . . ." Smart, *Viva Juárez!* 47.
p. 37, "[They] could only say . . ." Tamayo, *Antología de Benito Juárez*, 6.
p. 39, "Peoples who are . . ." Justo Sierra, *The Political Evolution of the Mexican People* (Austin: University of Texas Press, 1969), 175.
p. 47, "He is very homely . . ." Smart, *Viva Juárez!* 69.

CHAPTER FOUR: Governor Juárez
p. 48, "Our population is . . ." *The Annals of America 1841-1849*, vol. 7, "Manifest Destiny" (Chicago: Encyclopedia Britannica, Inc., 1976), 36.
p, 53, "Green grow the lilacs . . ." Ibid, 373.
p. 56, "The Mexican soldier . . ." Sierra, *The Political Evolution of the Mexican People*, 241-242.
p. 56, "we are called upon . . ." Smart, *Viva Juárez!* 89.
p. 56, "He [Juarez] could not forgive . . ." Ibid., 61.
p. 58, "The United States took . . ." Octavio Paz, *The Labyrinth of Solitude* (New York: Grove Press, 1961), 124.
p. 59, "I am the son . . ." Krause, *Mexico: Biography of Power*, 167.
p. 60, "in order to give . . ." Smart, Viva Juárez! 45.
p. 60, "To form women . . ." Ibid., 93.
p. 63, "We have a fundamental . . ." Ibid., 89.

CHAPTER FIVE: Juárez and the Reform
p, 72, "Because, what importance . . ." Smart, *Viva Juárez!*, 118.

p. 73, "the memorable Plan of . . ." Angel Pola, ed., *Discursos y Manifiestas de Benito Juárez Tomo II* (Mexico: DF, Instituto Nacional de Estudios Historicos de la Revolucion Mexicana, 1987), 22.

p. 75, ""Mexico was born . . ." Paz, Octavio. *The Labyrinth of Solitude* (New York, Grove Press, 1961), 127

p. 79, "precious fruit the people . . ." Pola, *Discursos y Manifiestas*, 22.

CHAPTER SIX: A Besieged Presidency

p. 81, "The abominable custom . . ." Sierra, *The Political Evolution of the Mexican People*, 286.

p. 81, "For good measure . . ." Ibid.

p. 84, "Put up your arms . . ." Smart, *Viva Juárez!* 174.

p. 84, "my heart broke out . . ." Ibid., 175.

p, 86, "to carry out the law . . .." Tamayo, *Antología de Benito Juárez*, 21.

p. 86, "The Indians are spread . . ." Gilbert M. Joseph and Timothy J. Henderson, eds., *The Mexico Reader* (Durham and London: Duke University Press, 2002), 227.

p. 92, "The Reform movement . . ." Paz, *The Labyrinth of Solitude*, 126.

p. 92, "Nothing by force . . ." T. R. Fehrenbach, *Fire and Blood: A History of Mexico* (New York: Macmillan, 1973), 422.

CHAPTER SEVEN: The French Intervention

p. 97, "A foreign monarchy . . ." Joan Haslip, *The Crown of Mexico* (New York: Holt, Rinehart, and Winston, 1971), 183.

p. 98, "We are so superior . . ." Fehrenbach, *Fire and Blood: A History of Mexico*, 423.

p. 99, "Your enemies are . . ." Ibid., 428.

CHAPTER EIGHT: The Crown of Mexico

p. 108, "Do not trust . . ." Jasper Ridley, *Maximilian and Juárez* (New York: Tichnor & Fields, 1992), 5.

p. 109, "[Those who] attack the rights . . ." Henry Bamford Parkes, *A History of Mexico* (Boston: Houghton Mifflin Company, 1969), 261.

p. 109, "Long live the Republic . . ." Ridley, *Maximilian and Juárez*, 165.

p. 111, "With his slender . . ." Sierra, *The Political Evolution of the Mexican People*, 324.

p. 111-112, "It [will be] the . . ." Krause, *Mexico: Biography of Power*, 177.

p. 112, "At a trot . . ." Adams, Jerome R. *Latin American Heros* (New York, Ballantine Books, 1991), 146

p. 115, "The Institution of monarchy . . ." Joseph and Henderson, *The Mexico Reader*, 264.

CHAPTER NINE: The Fall of the Crown

p. 119, "Mexico owes her independence . . ." Haslip, *The Crown of Mexico*, 298.

p. 120, "Mexicans after three years . . ." Pola, *Discursos y Manifiestas*, 276.

p. 122, "The best are and . . ." Krause, *Mexico: Biography of Power*, 182.

p. 123, "To come to me . . ." Ibid., 184.

p. 123, "The time for indulgence . . ." Ridley, *Maximilian and Juárez*, 228.

p. 125, "Moral resistance to the . . ." Sierra, *The Political Evolution of the Mexican People*, 331.

p. 126, "The ship sails . . ." Krause, Mexico: *Biography of Power*, 187.

p. 127, "To me he is . . ." Ridley, *Maximilian and Juárez*, 248.

p. 130, "I am not . . ." Krause, *Mexico: Biography of Power*, 191.

p. 131, "He already seemed . . ." Haslip, *The Crown of Mexico*, 497.

p. 132, "one is . . ." Ridley, *Maximilian and Juárez*, 290.

CHAPTER TEN: The Father of the Country

p. 134, "Mexicans: we have . . ." Pola, *Discursos y Manifiestas*, 290.

p. 134, "The country was a . . ." Sierra, *The Political Evolution of the Mexican People*, 357.

p. 134, "For me it is . . ." Smart, *Viva Juárez!* 386.

p. 138, "The urban masses . . ." Sierra, *The Political Evolution of the Mexican People*, 357.

p. 134, "I would like to see . . ." Ibid., 348.

p. 134, "We have never seen . . ." Smart, *Viva Juárez!* 406.

p. 140, "Indefinate reelections . . ." Fehrenbach, *Fire and Blood: A History of Mexico*, 449.

p. 140, "Once again he . . ." Sierra, *The Political Evolution of the Mexican People*, 350.

p. 142, "Is my illness . . ." Smart, *Viva Juárez!* 417.

Bibliography

Adams, Jerome R. *Latin American Heroes.* New York: Ballantine Books, 1991.

Fehrenbach, T.R. *Fire and Blood: A History of Mexico.* New York: Macmillan, 1973.

Gilbert M. Joseph and Timothy J. Henderson, eds. *The Mexico Reader: History, Culture, Politics.* Durham and London: Duke University Press, 2002.

Haslip, Joan. *The Crown of Mexico.* New York: Holt, Rinehart, and Winston, 1971.

Kandell, Jonathan. *La Capital: The Biography of Mexico City.* New York: Random House, 1988.

Krause, Enrique. *Mexico: Biography of Power.* New York: Harper Collins, 1997.

Parkes, Henry Bamford. *A History of Mexico.* Boston: Houghton Mifflin Company, 1969.

Paz, Octavio. *The Labyrinth of Solitude.* New York: Grove Press, 1961.

Pola, Angel, compilador. *Discursos y Manifiestas de Benito Juárez Tomo II.* Mexico: Instituto Nacional de Estudios Historicos de la Revolucion Mexicana, 1987.

Ridley, Jasper, *Maximilian and Juárez*. New York: Tichnor & Fields, 1992.

Roeder, Ralph, *Juarez and His Mexico*. New York: The Viking Press, 1947.

Sierra, Justo, *The Political Evolution of the Mexican People*. Austin: University of Texas Press, 1969.

Smart, Charles Allen. *Viva Juárez!* New York: J. B. Lippincott Company, 1963.

Tamayo, Jorge L., ed. *Antología de Benito Juárez*. Mexico City, Universidad Nacional Autónoma de Mexico, 1972.

Web Sites

http://www.mexonline.com/benitojuarez.htm
The history of Benito Juárez

http://www.benitojuarez.org.ar/
Home Page de Benito Juárez (in Spanish)

http://www.britanica.com/eb/article-9044057/
Benito Juárez—Encyclopedia Britannica

1948 mural of Juárez (Courtesy of The Granger Collection)

Index